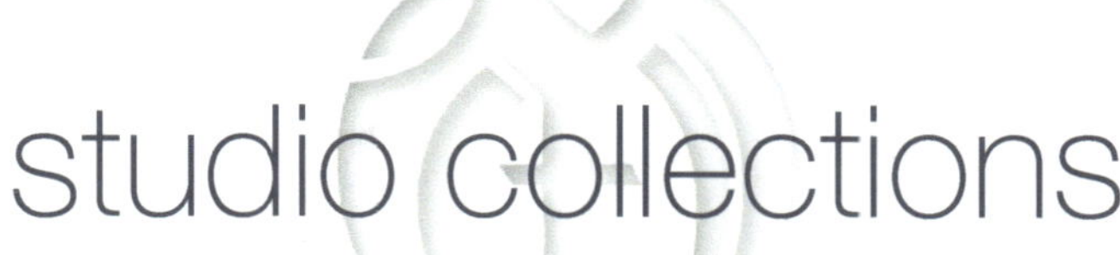

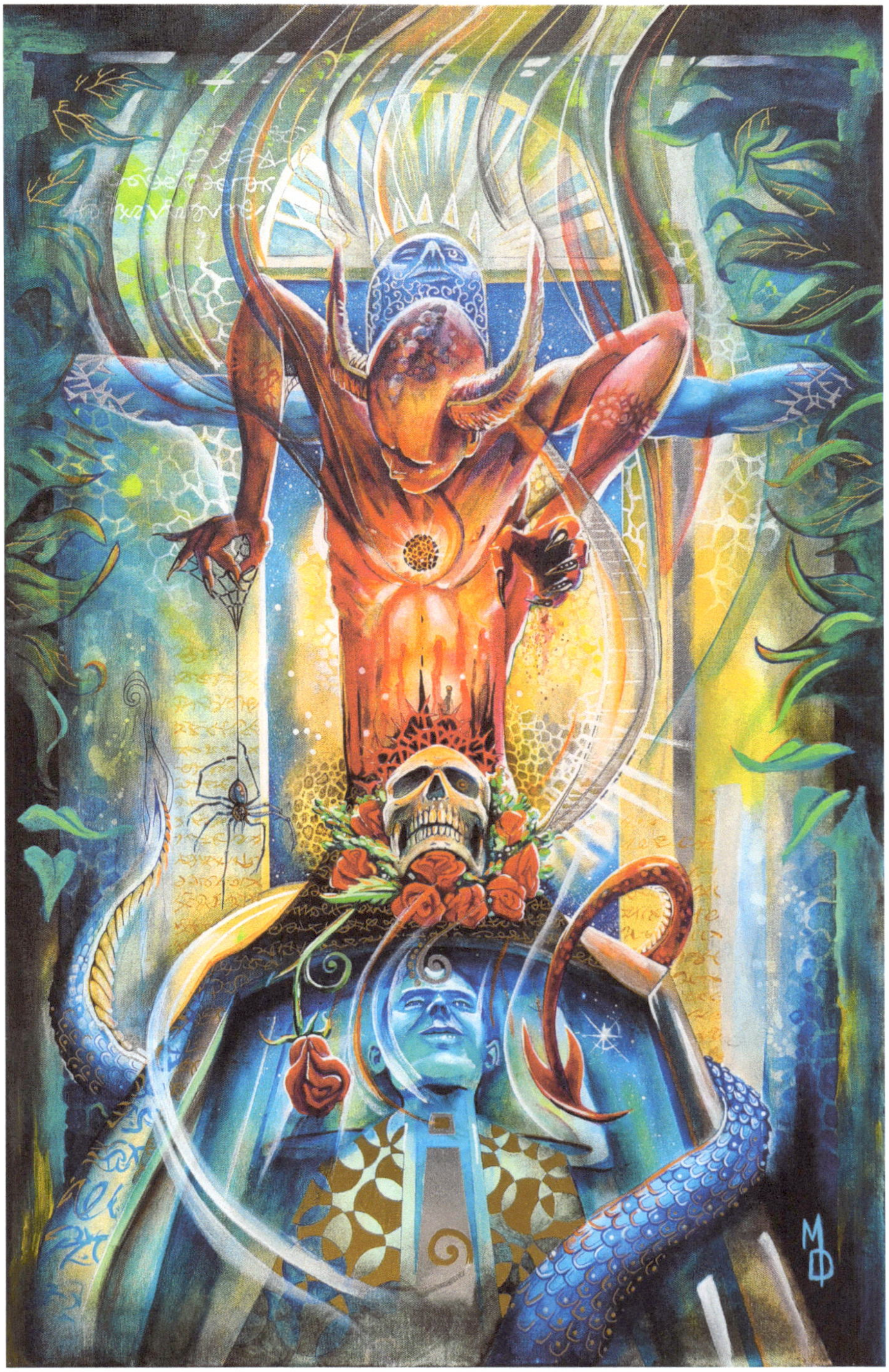

# Art by Miles Davis | Angels & Demons

Massive Burn Studios
www.massiveburn.com

First Edition 2024

ISBN 979-8-9918816-1-6

Artwork by Miles Davis
Cover Design and Typeset by Merissa Corbet Davis

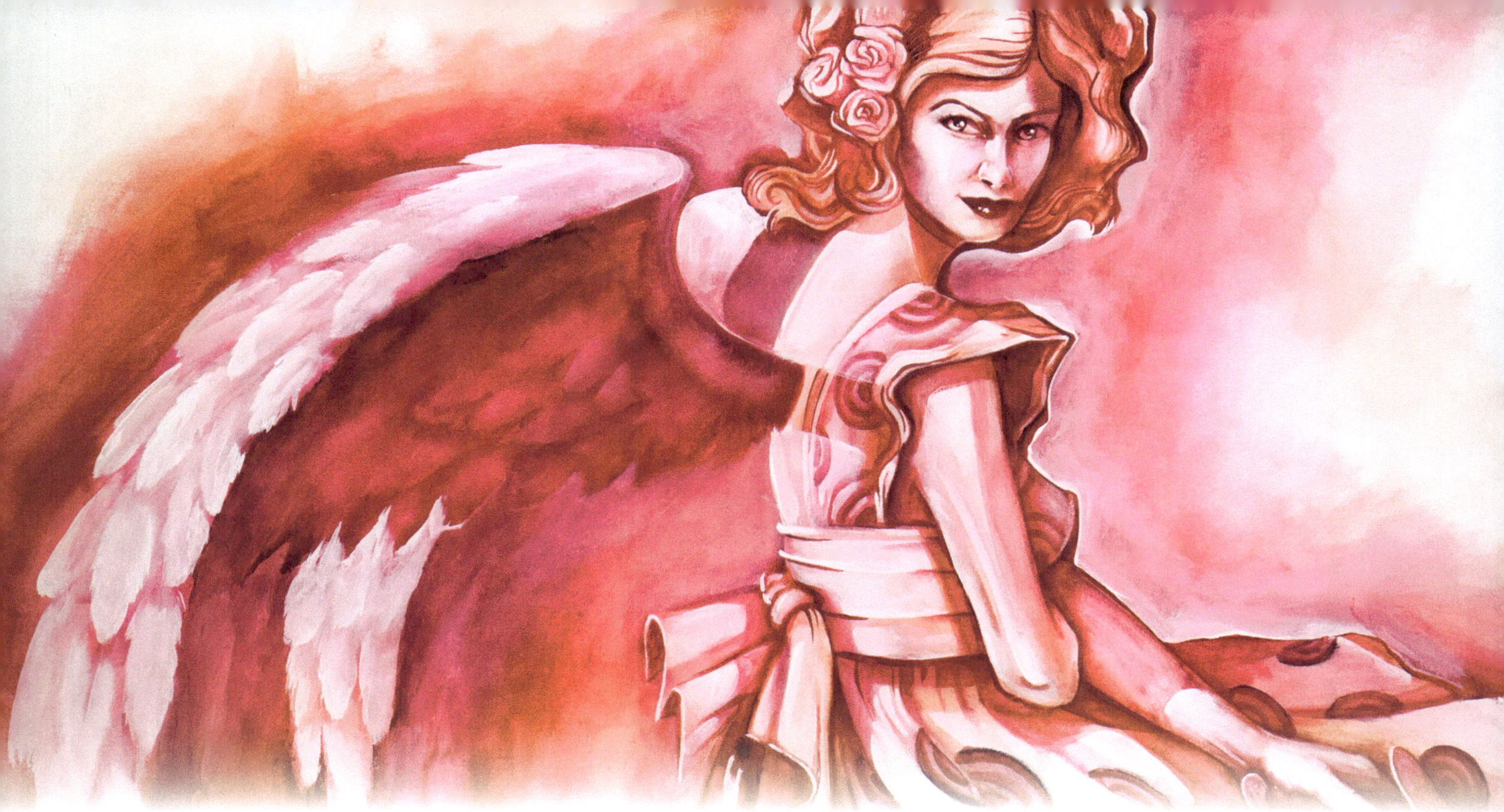

# Angels & Demons

Angels & Demons - the epitome of good and evil, light and dark, virtue and blasphemy. This hand-picked collection of imagery containing the common Western religious motifs explore the iconic symbolism, often re-imagined or stretched in an effort to express the duality of the human condition.

*Harvester of Knowledge*, 2021
30"x40"
Acrylic & Mixed Media, Gold Leaf on Canvas

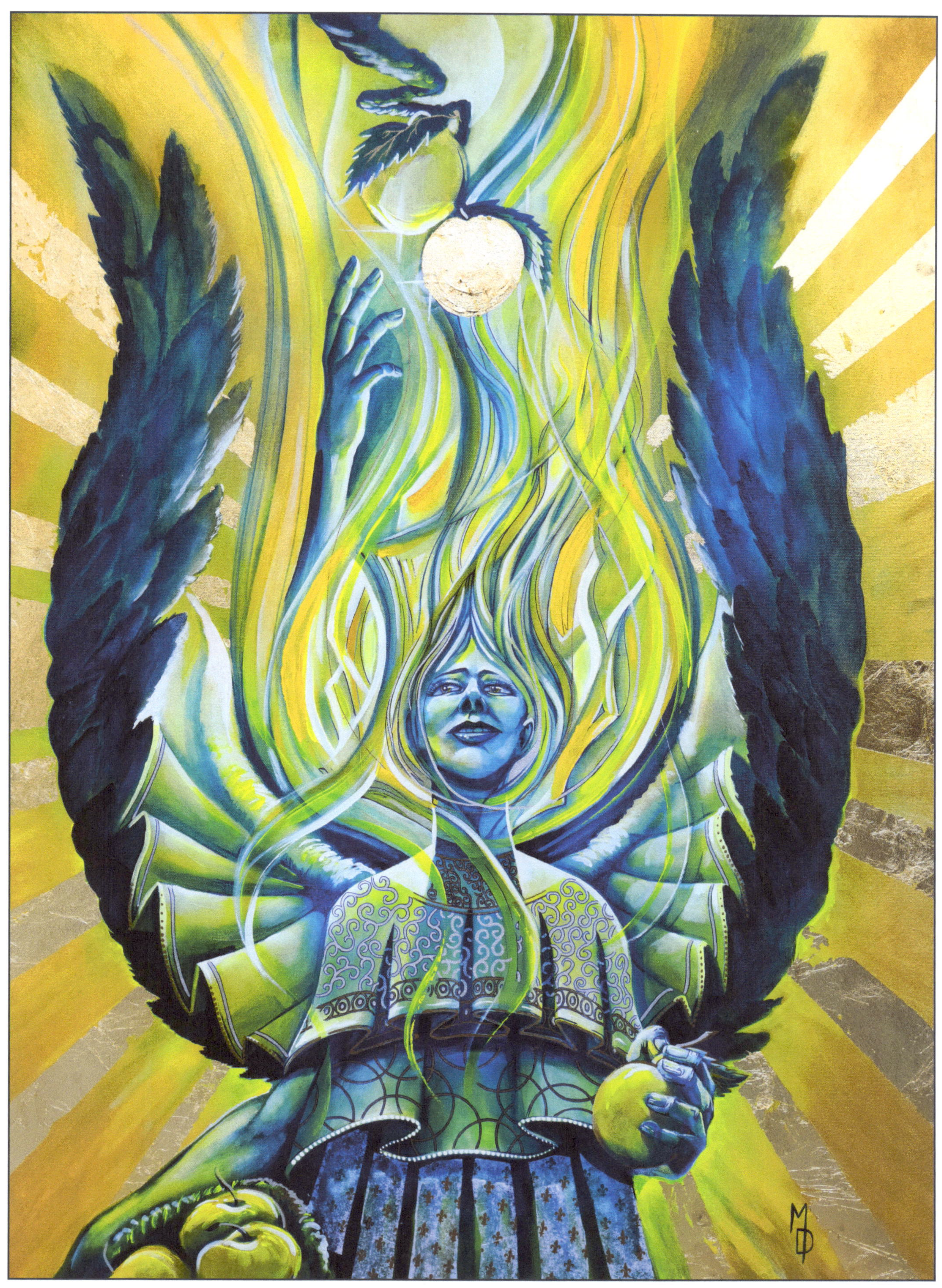

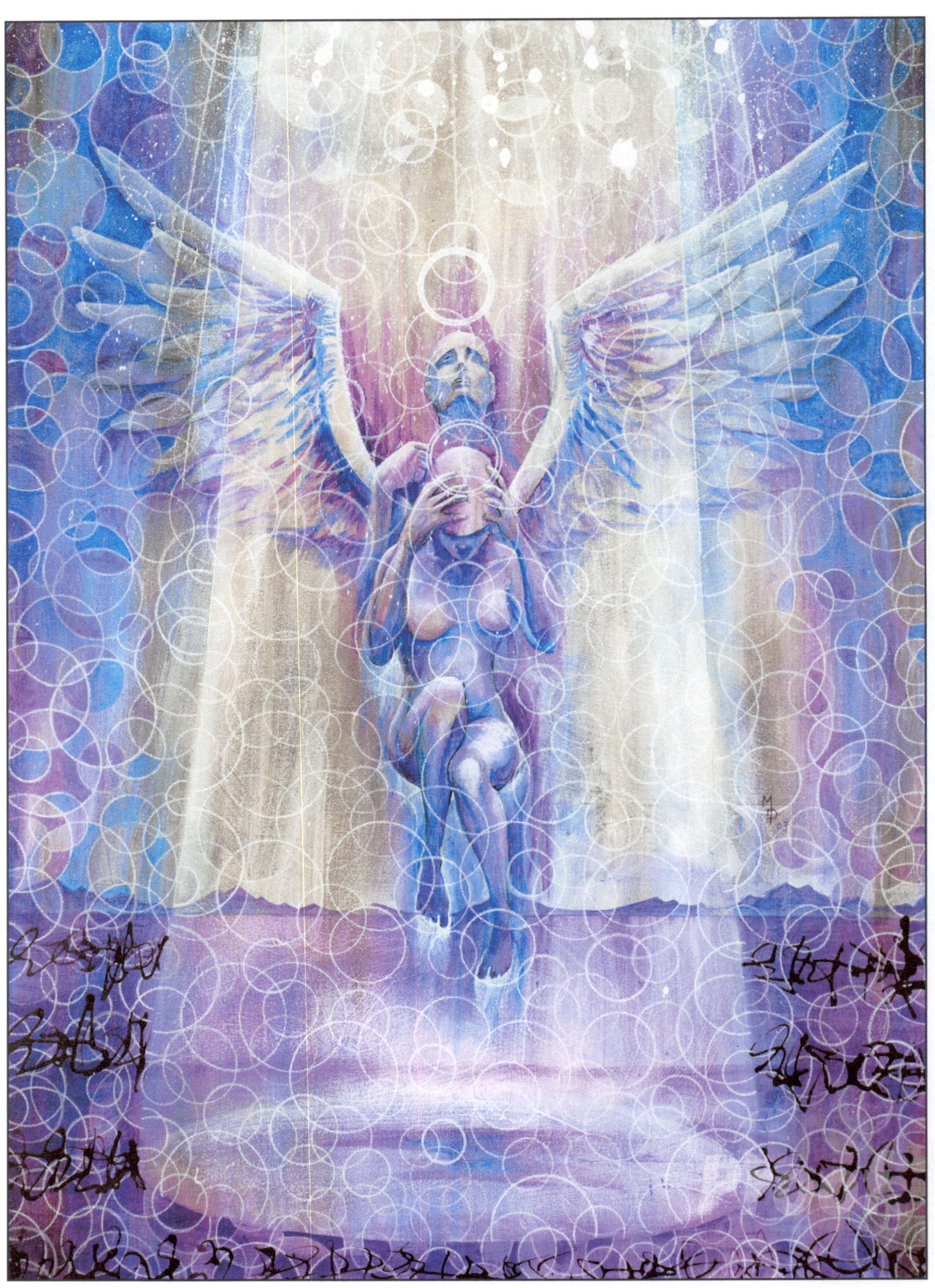

*Royal Regrets*, 2003
30"x40"
Acrylic & Mixed Media on Canvas

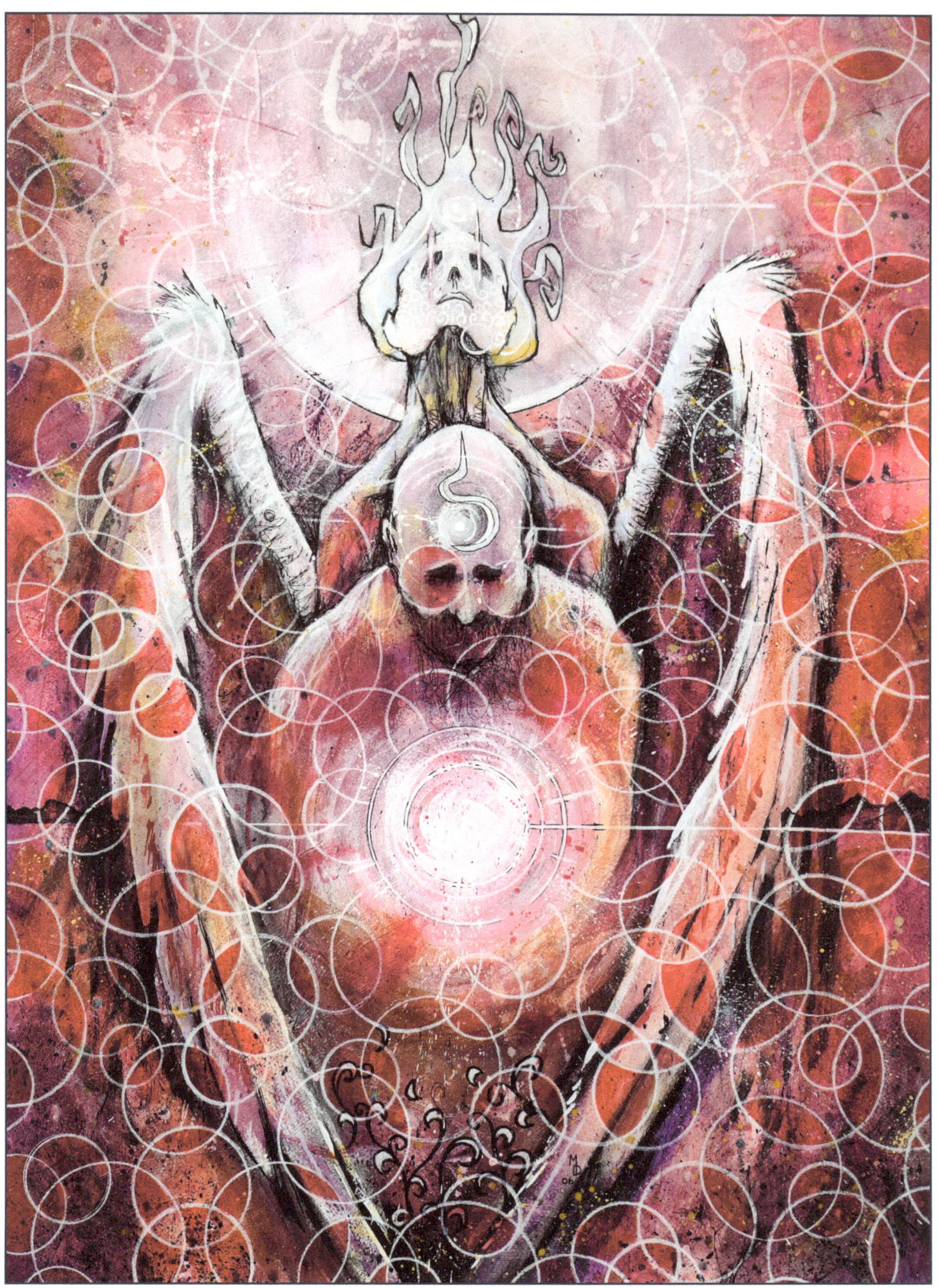

*Protection in Purgatory*, 2006
21"x29"
Acrylic & Mixed Media on Paper

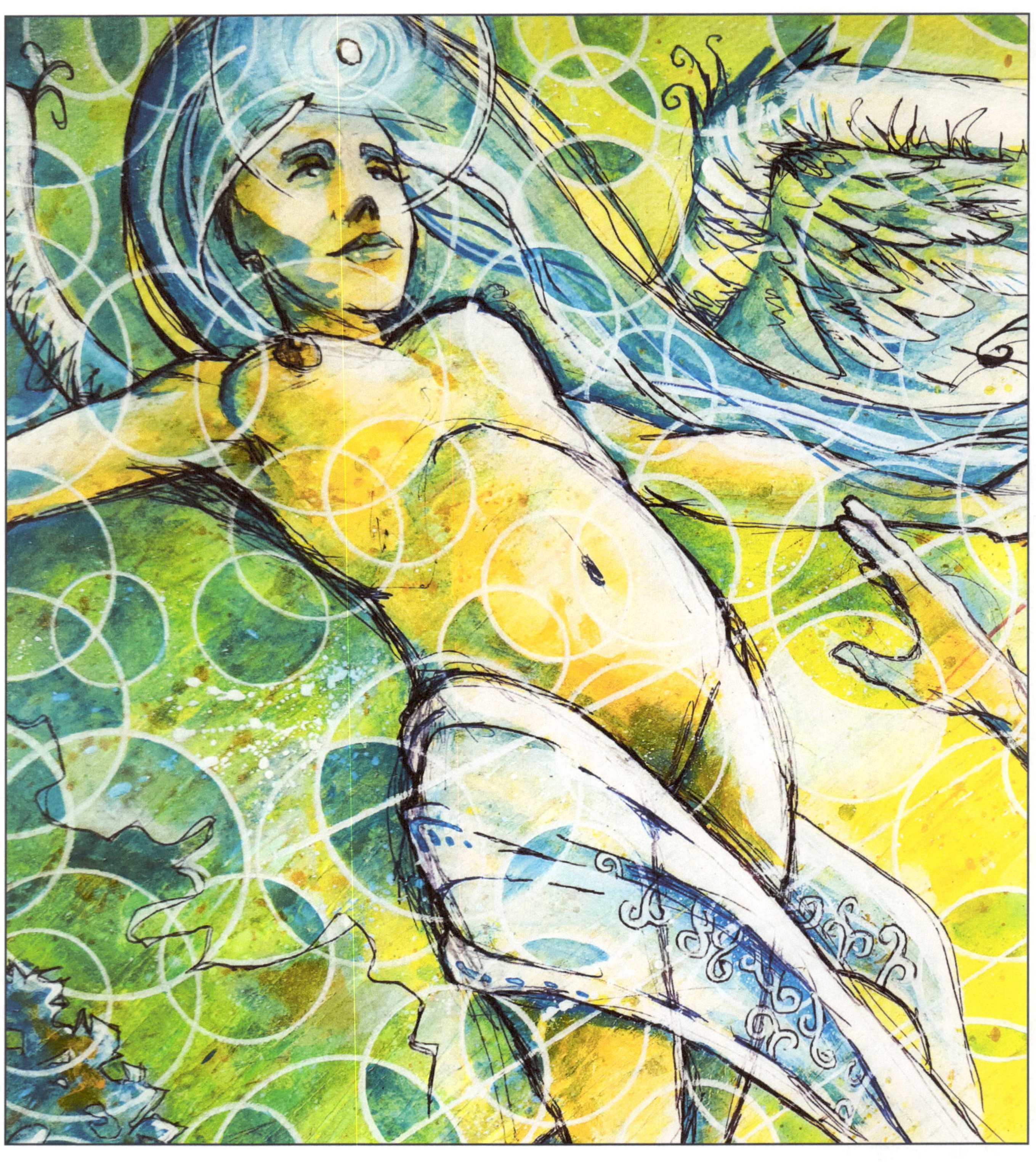

This woman borrows inspiration from *Medicine* (1900-1907) by Gustav Klimt.

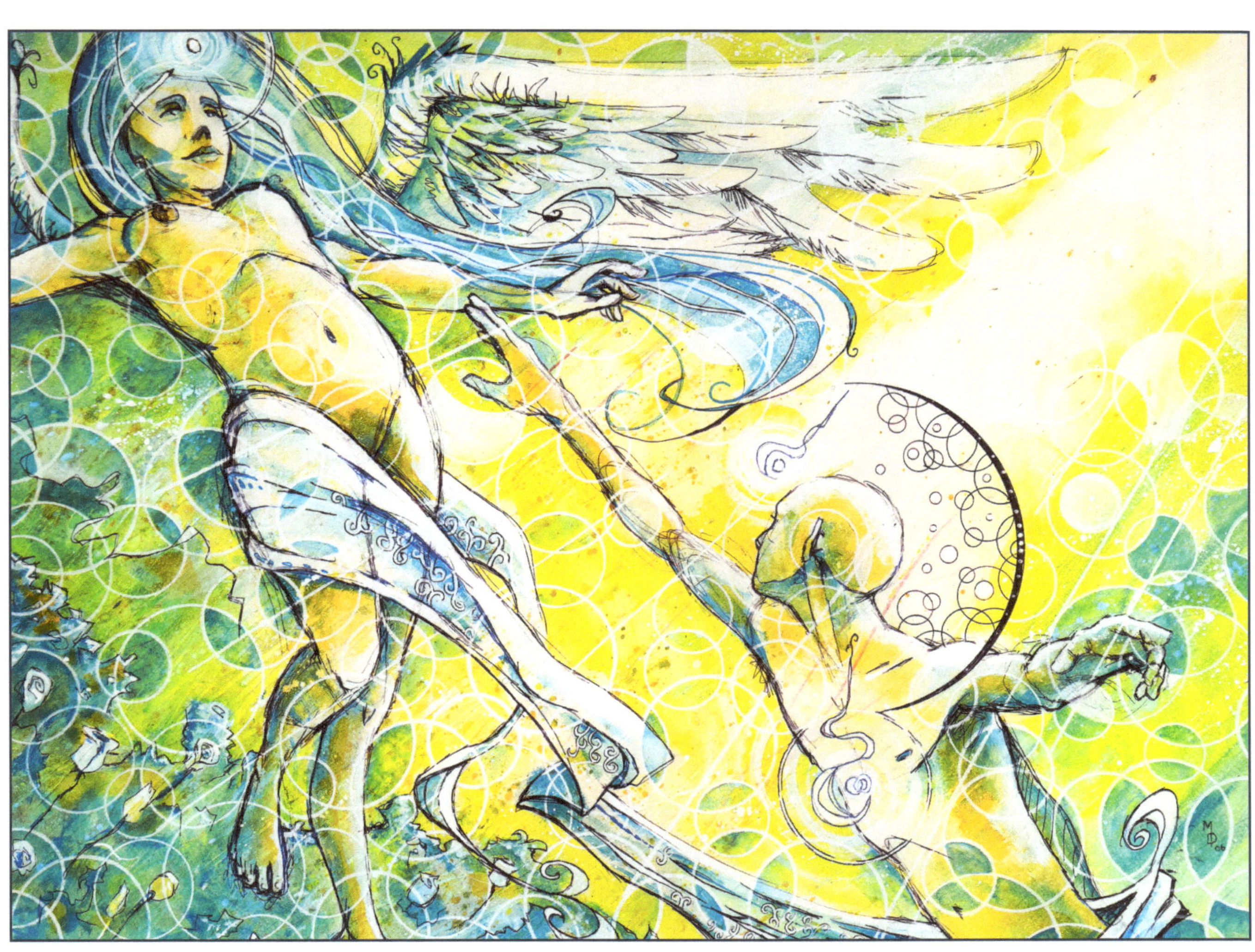

*Vigilance of Faith*, 2006
29"x21"
Acrylic & Mixed Media on Paper

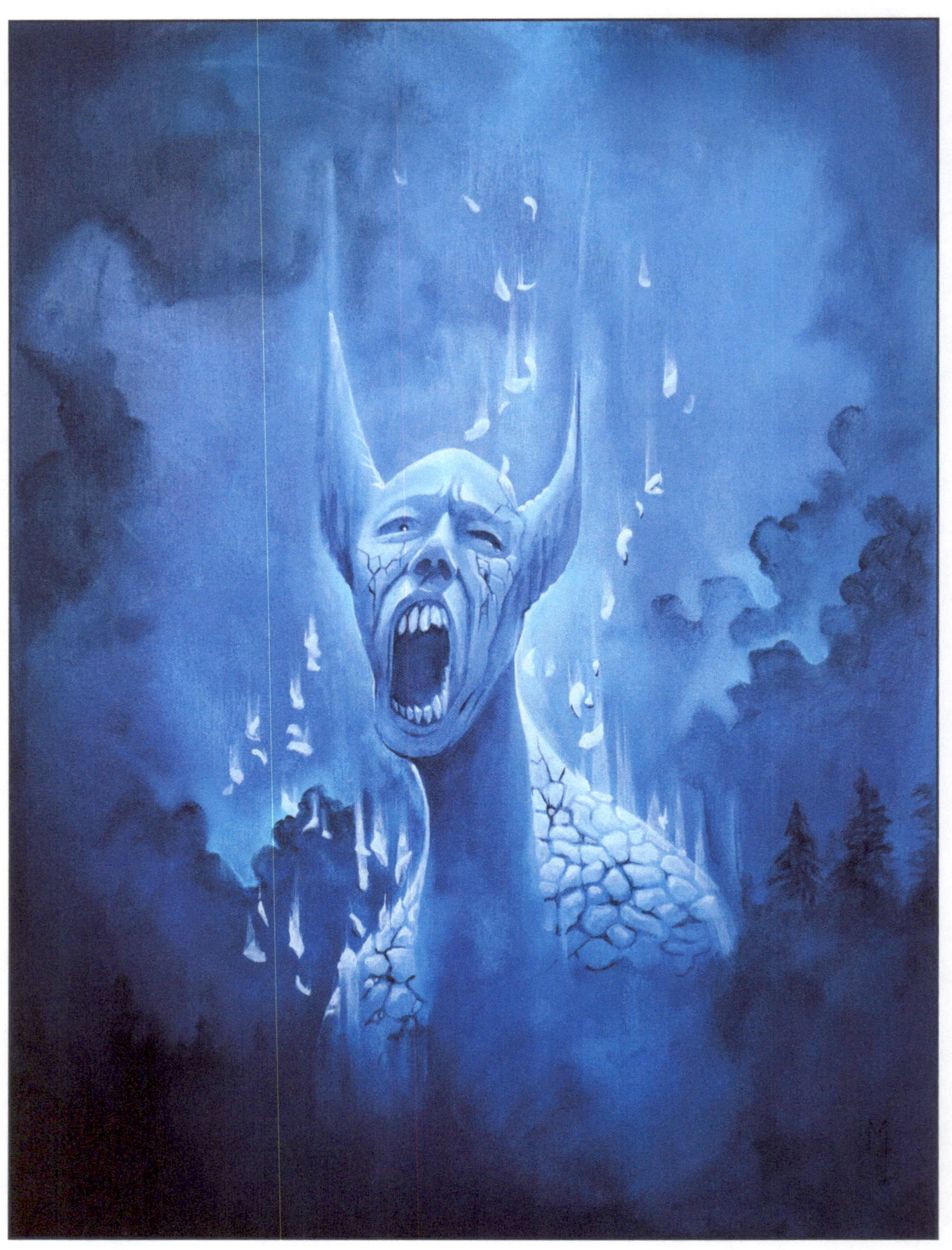

*Dissipate*, 2024
18"x24"
Acrylic & Mixed Media on Canvas

*Rhythms of Death*, 2022
24"x36"
Acrylic & Mixed Media on Canvas

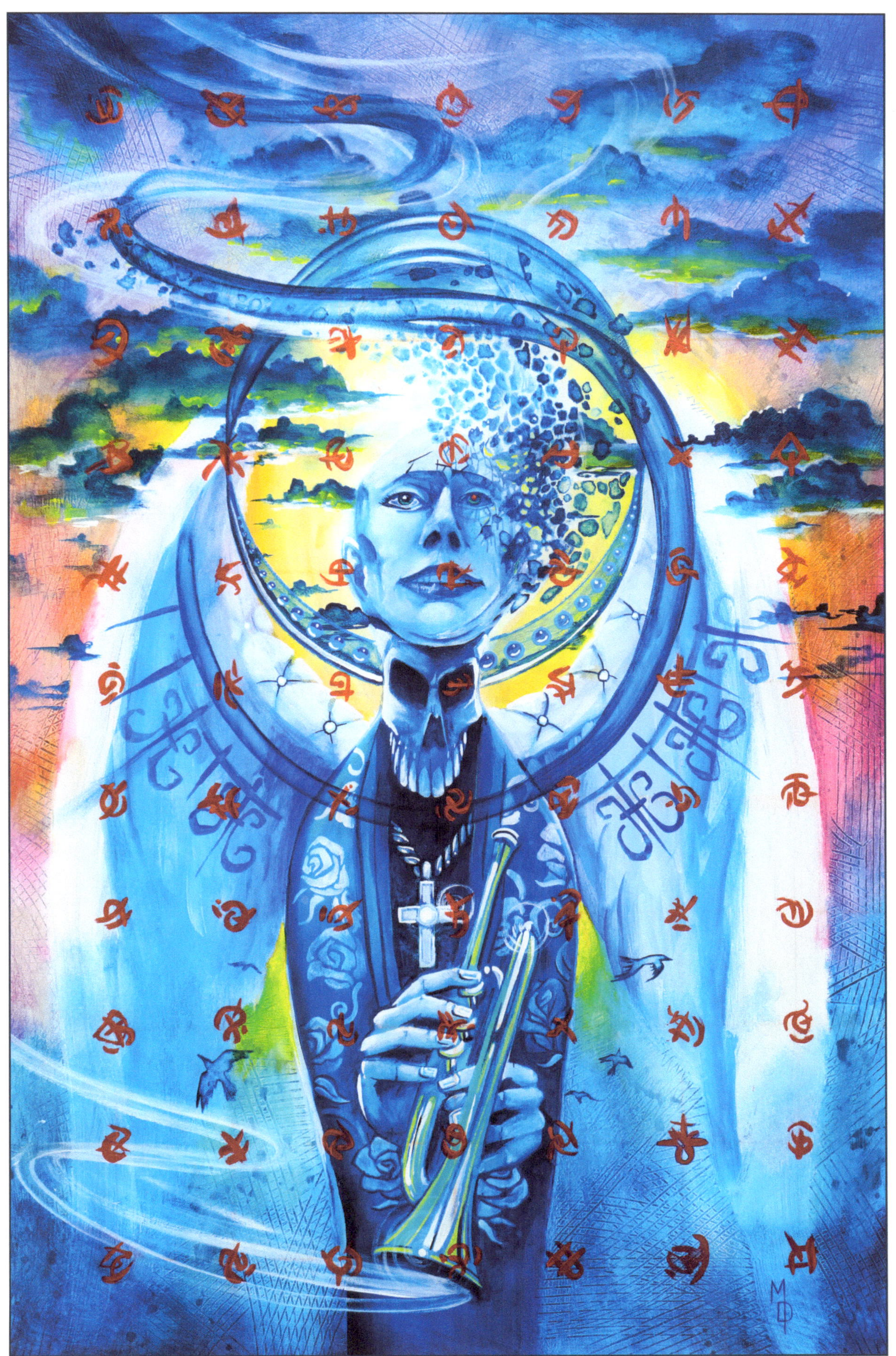

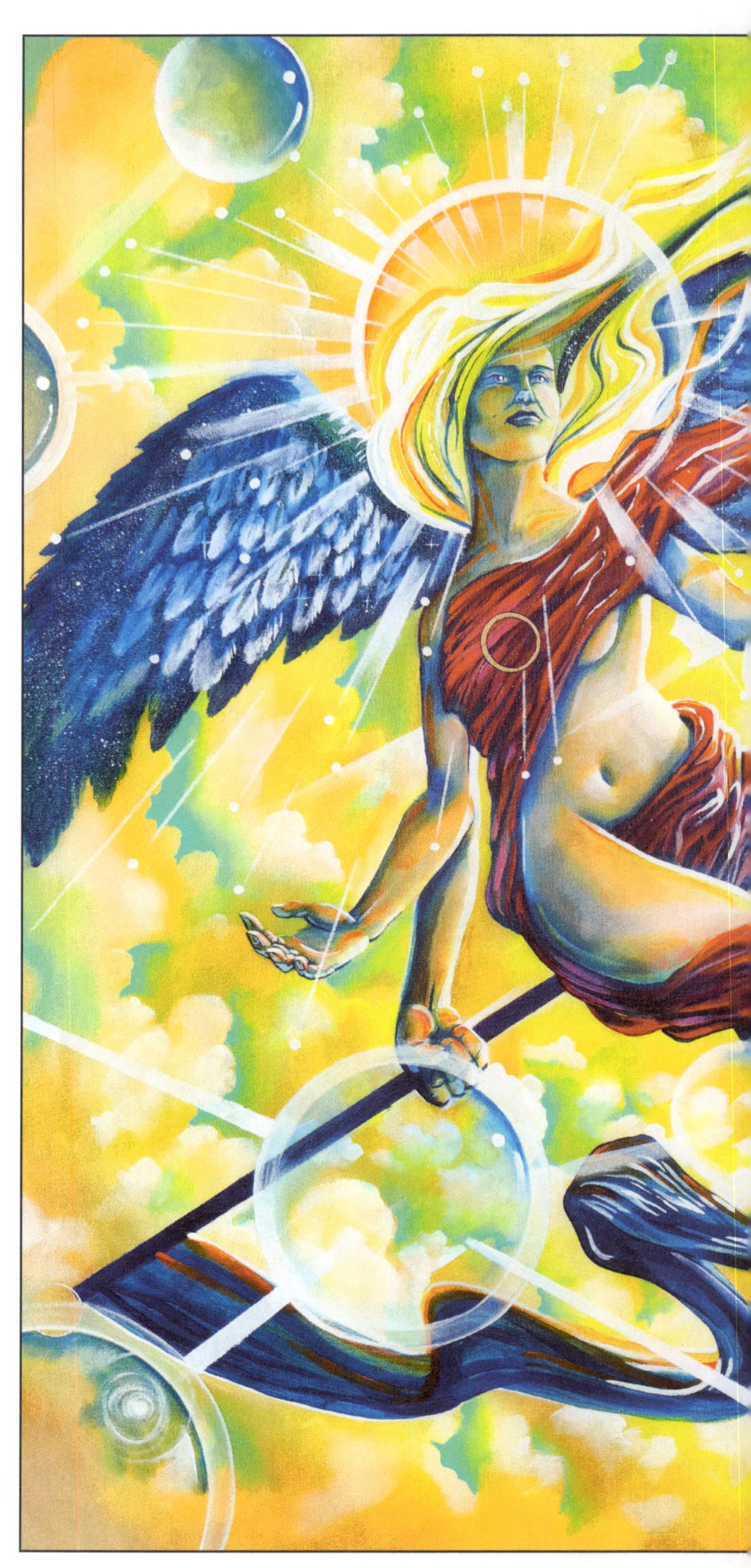

*Celestial Gifts*, 2021
48"x36"
Acrylic & Mixed Media on Canvas

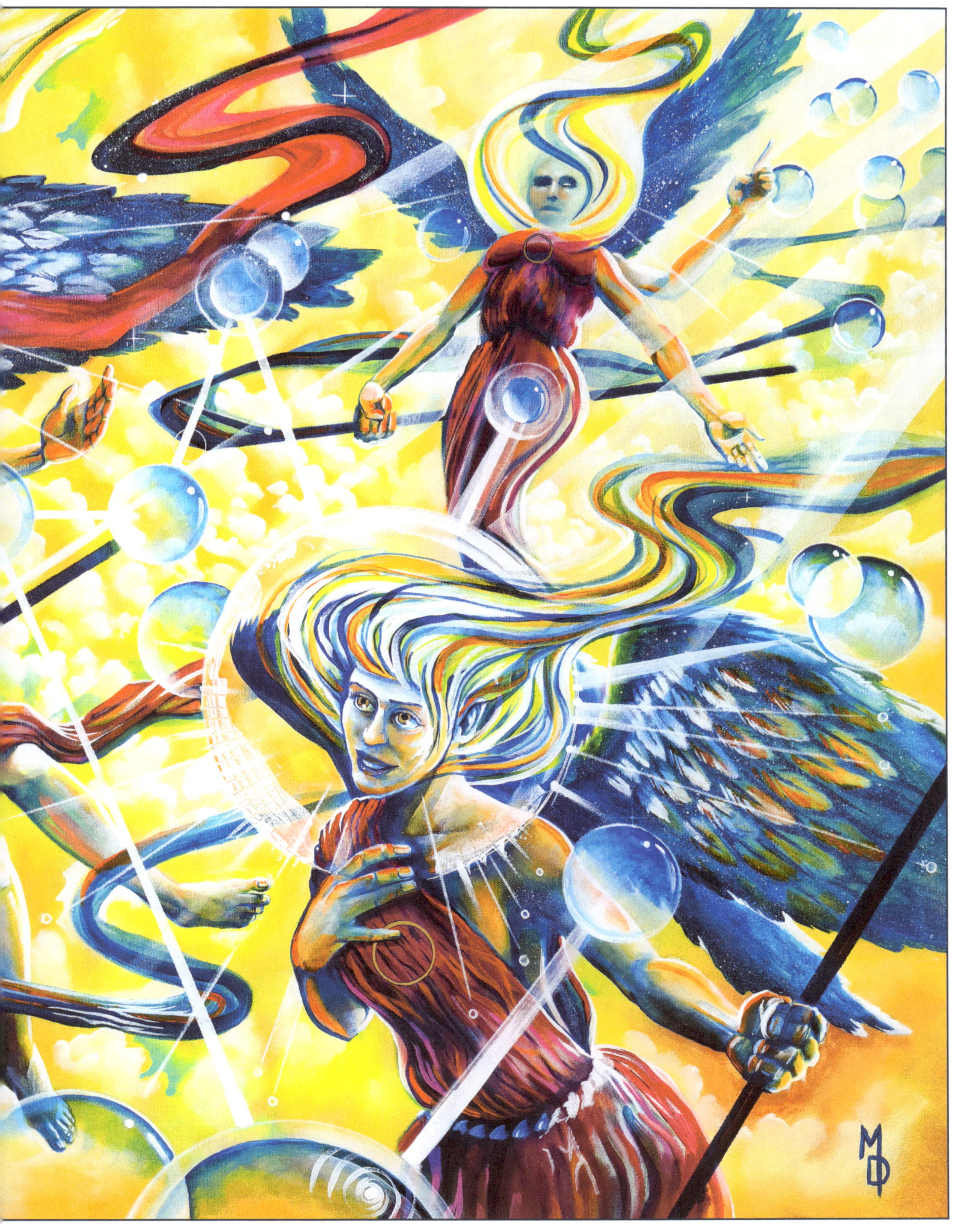

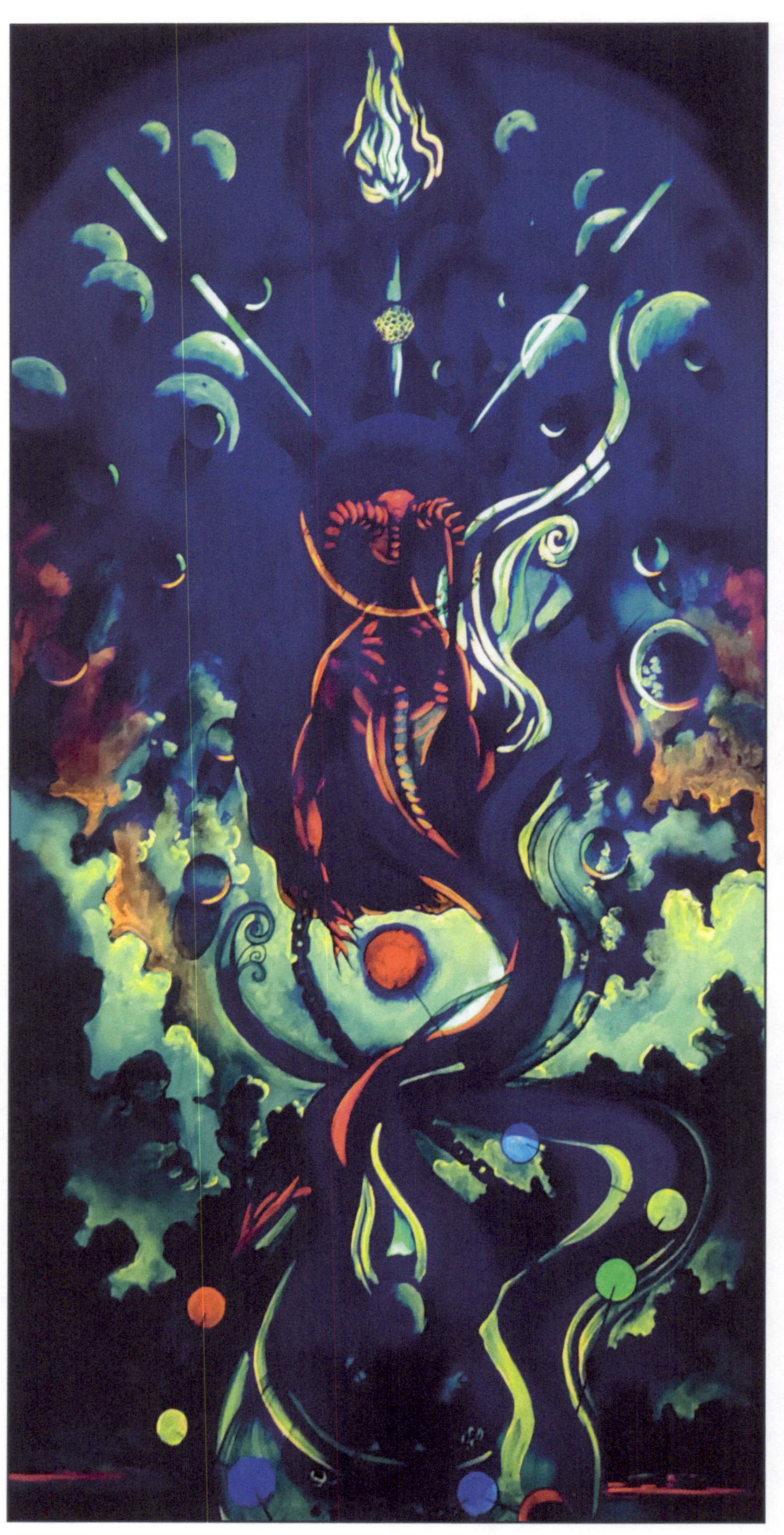

*Devil in the Details*, 2022
24"x48"
Acrylic & Mixed Media on Canvas
*Blacklight Enhanced*

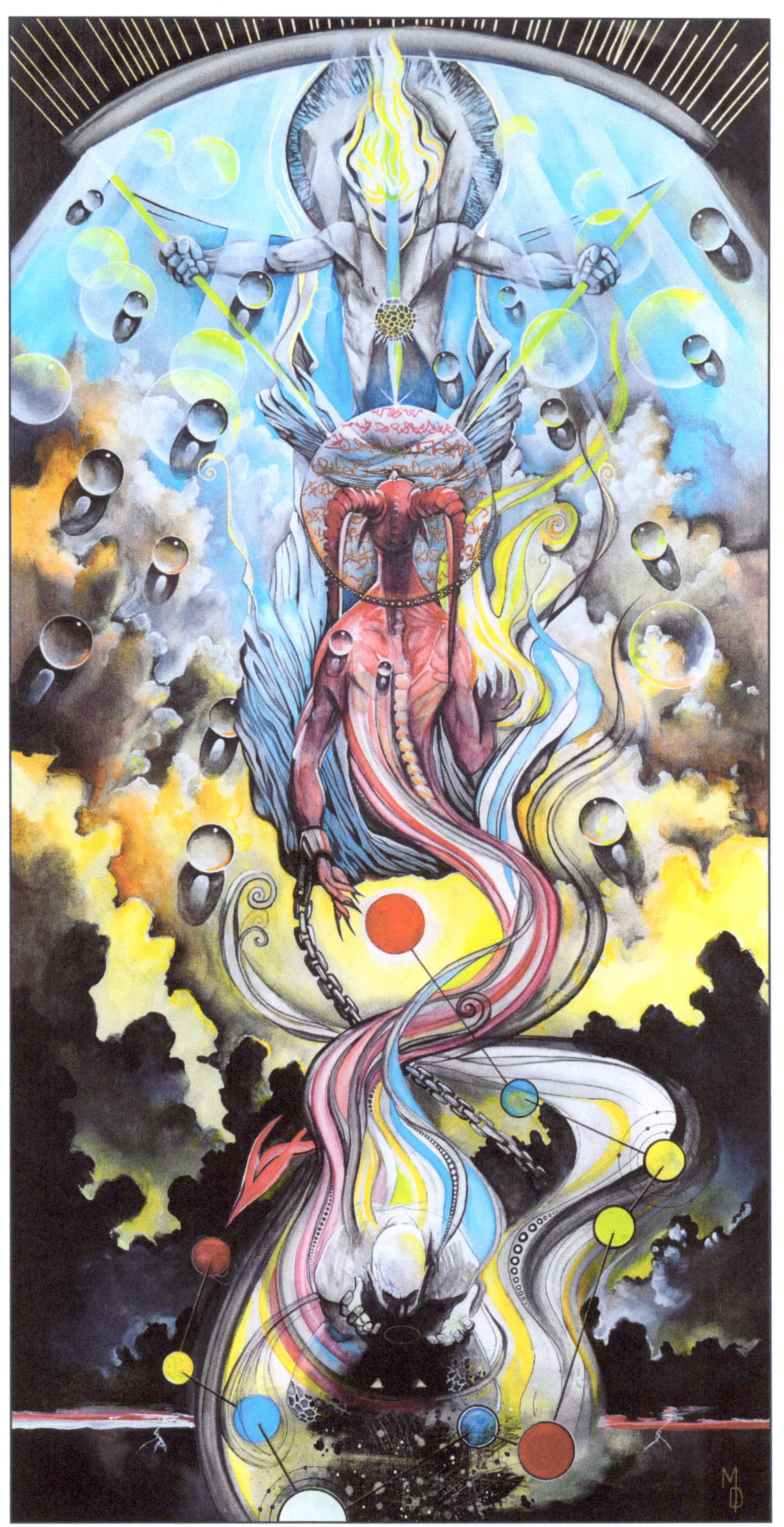

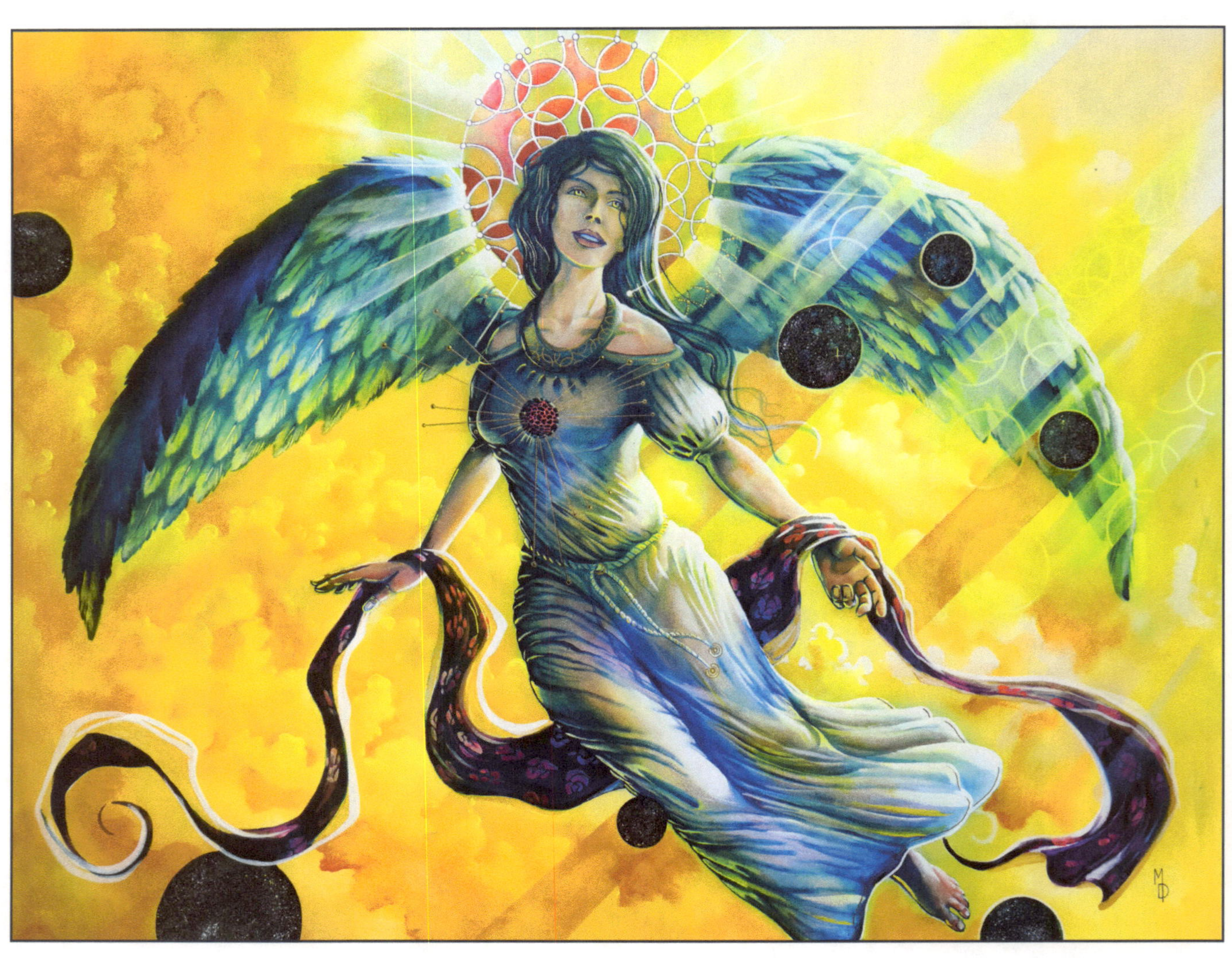

*Ethereal Angel*, 2020
48"x36"
Acrylic & Mixed Media on Canvas

*Prayers for the Dying*, 2017
30"x40"
Acrylic & Mixed Media on Canvas
*Blacklight Enhanced*

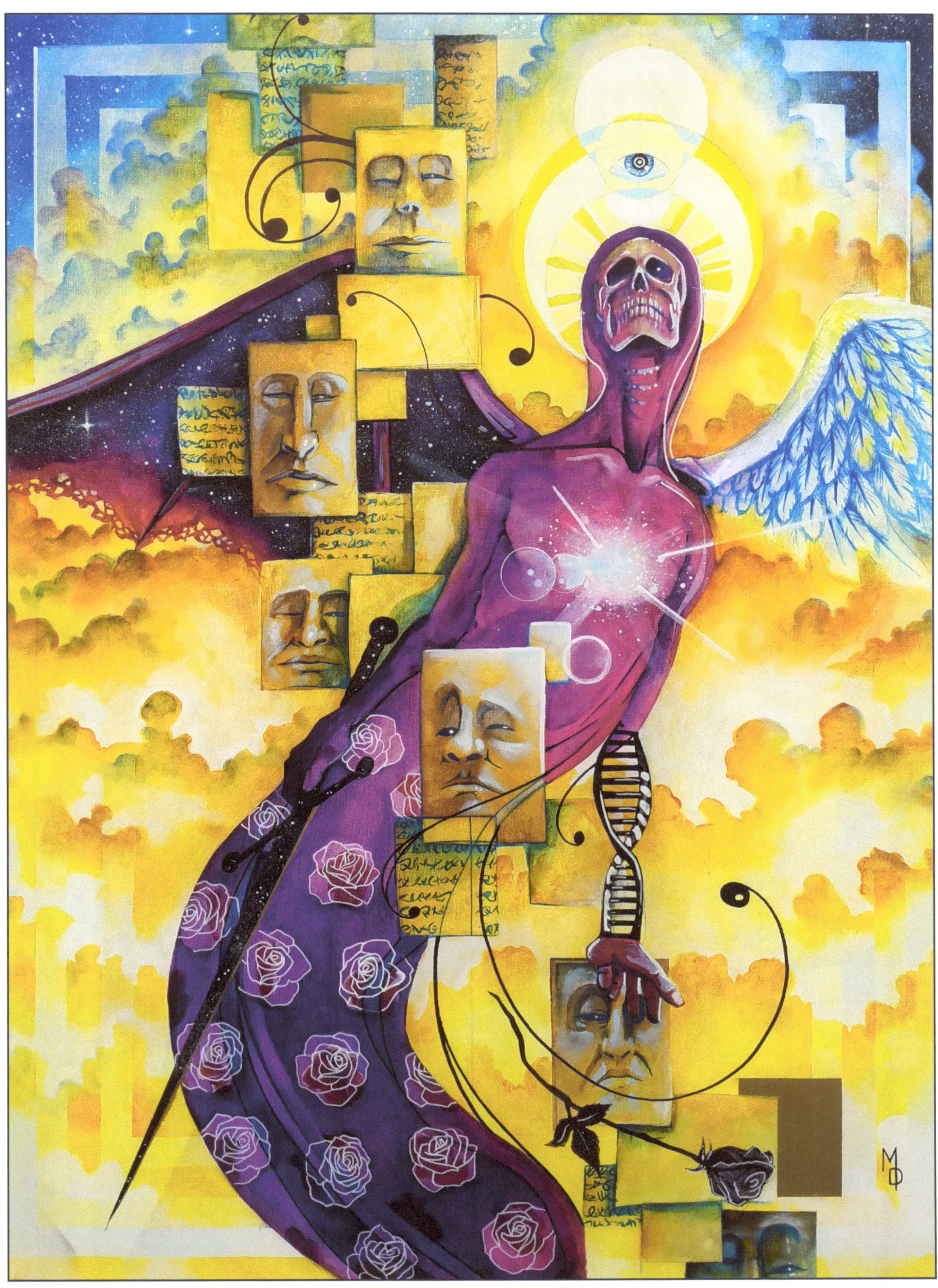

"This piece explores the battle between the id and the ego, self confidence and self doubt, the two sides of every coin."

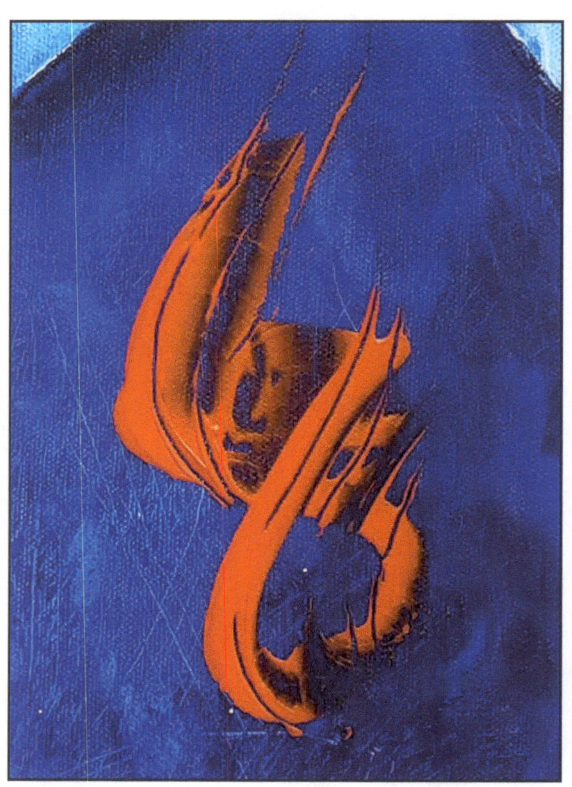

*Face Off*, 2019
24"x36"
Acrylic & Mixed Media on Canvas

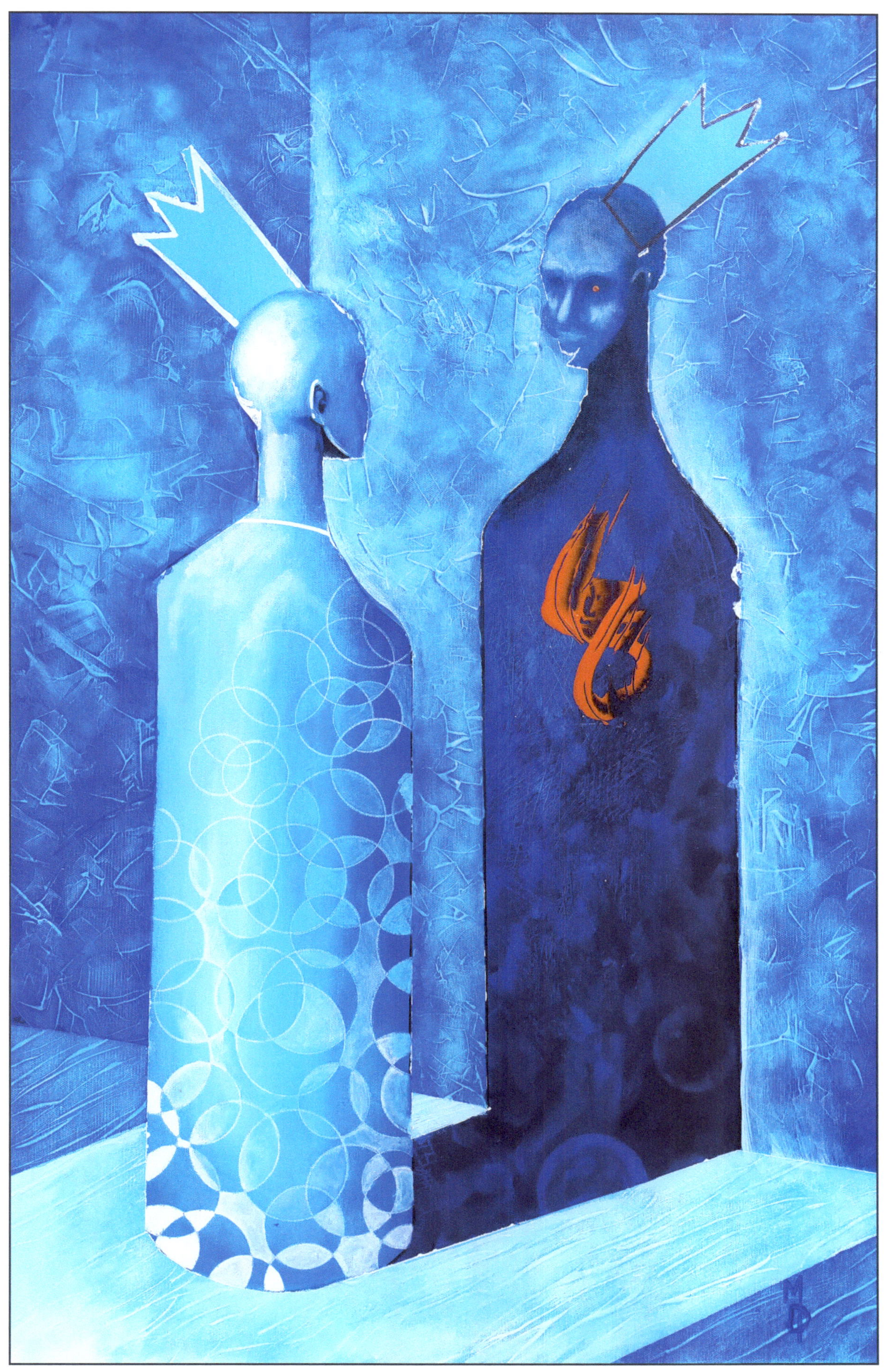

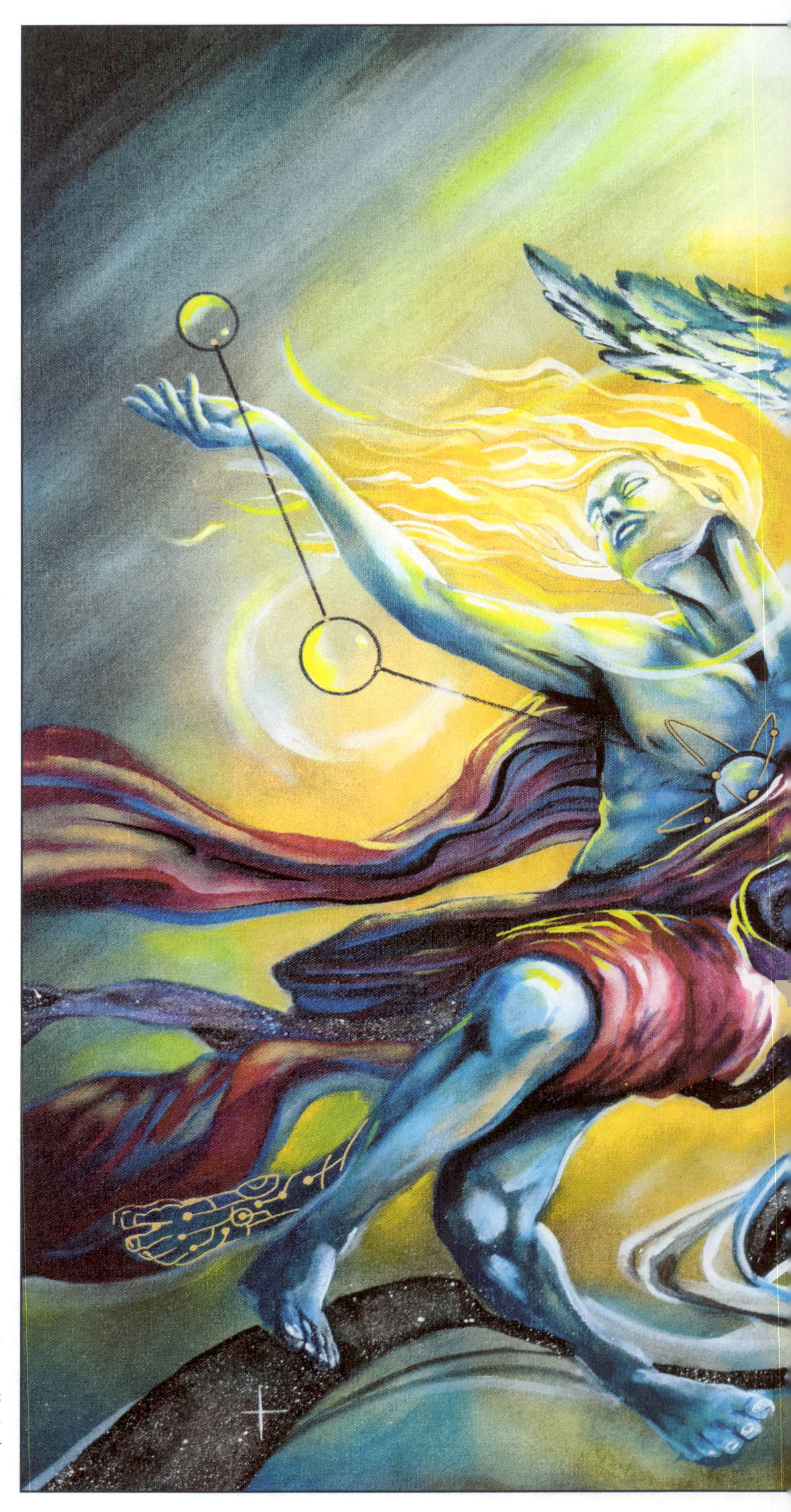

*Faith & Wisdom*, 2021
40"x30"
Acrylic & Mixed Media,
Gold Leaf on Canvas
*In the Permanent Collection of the*
*Marietta Cobb Museum of Art*

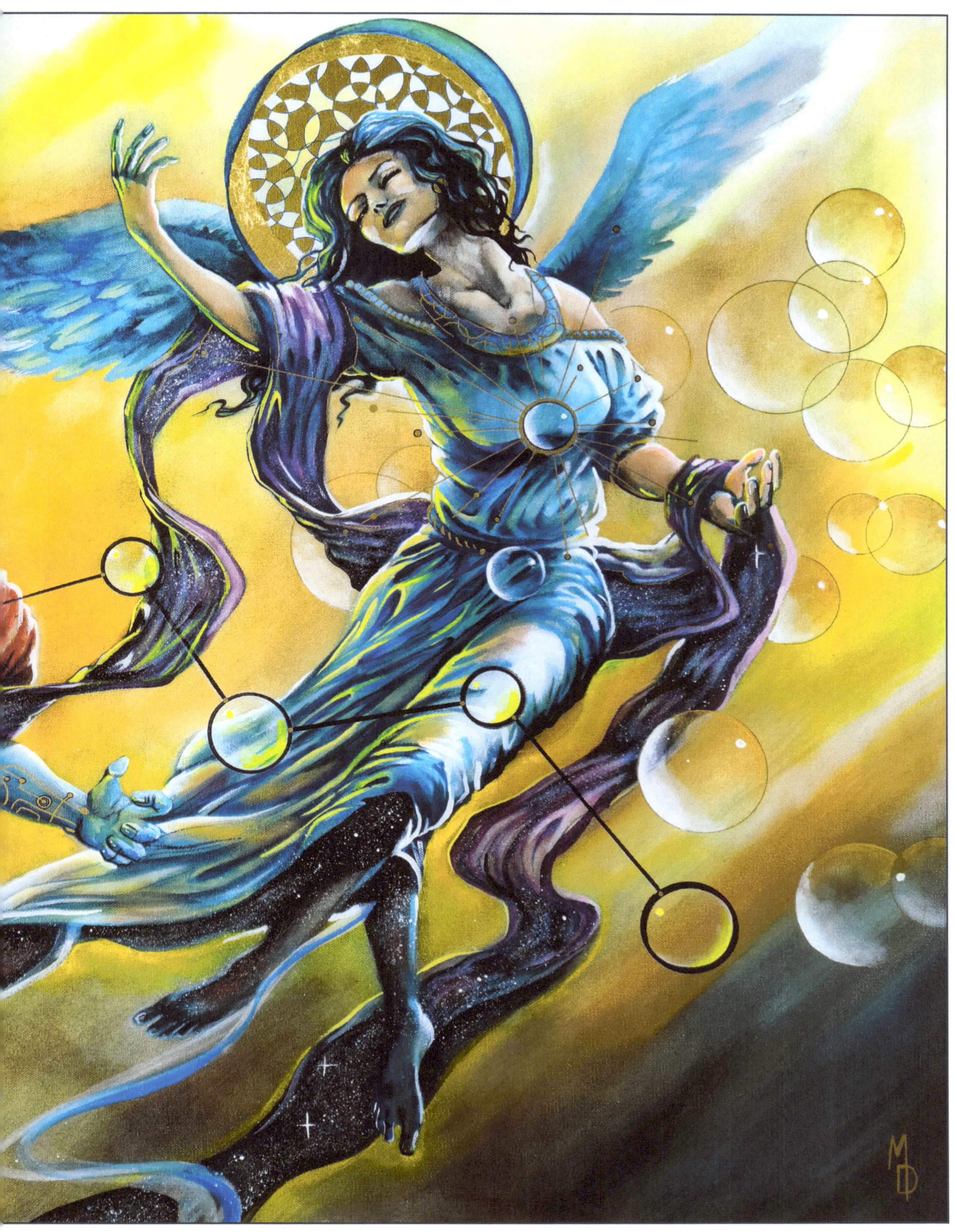

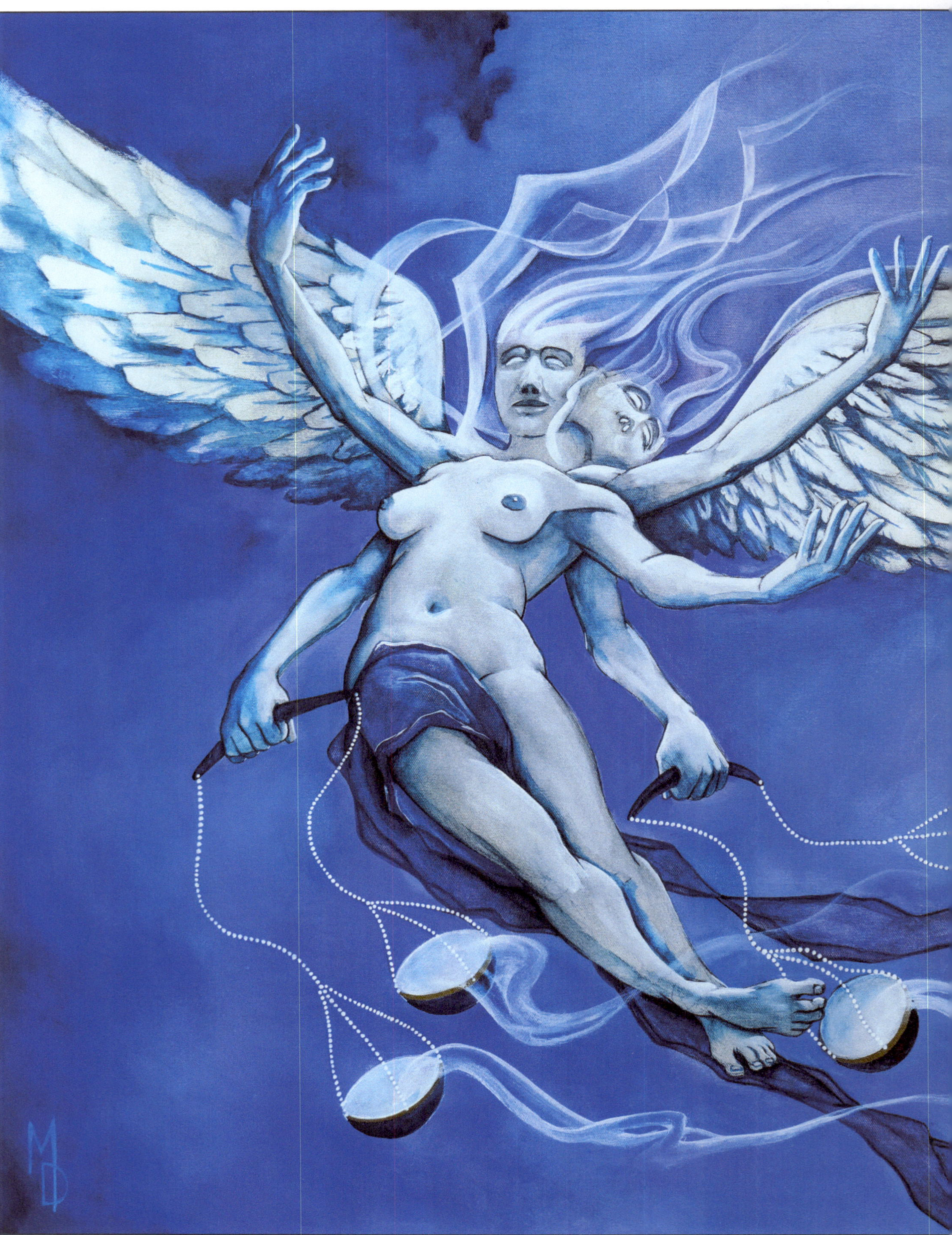

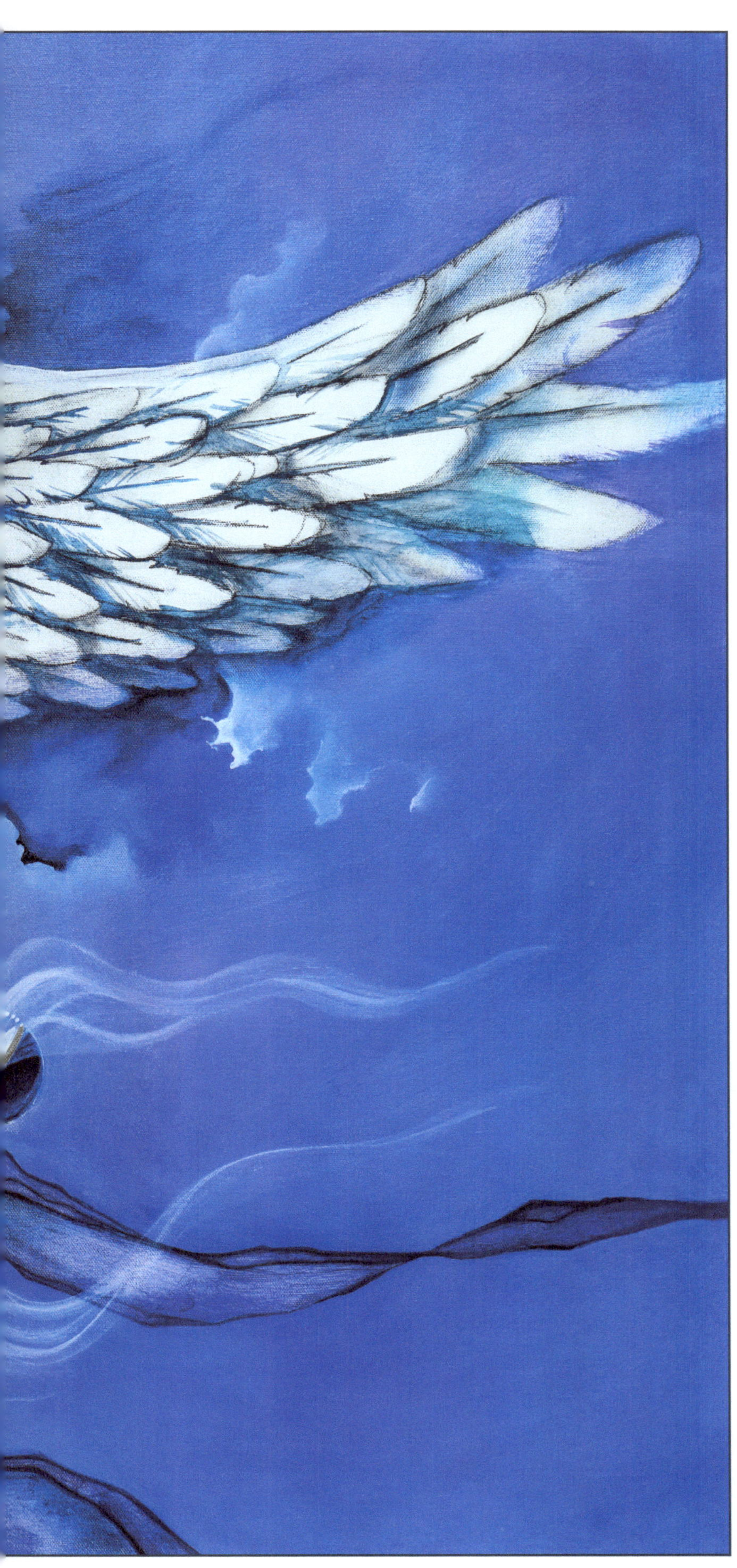

*Retribution*, 2023
40"x30"
Acrylic & Mixed Media on Canvas

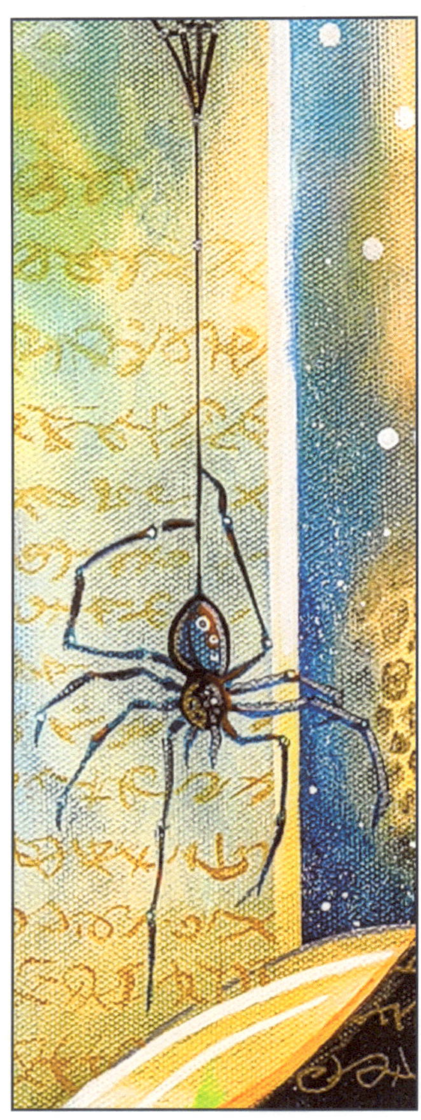

"*Atonement* was a tedious piece that remained very organic and changed directions a few times in process. Ultimately, I blended those elements into a cohesive narrative of the 'devil's due.'"

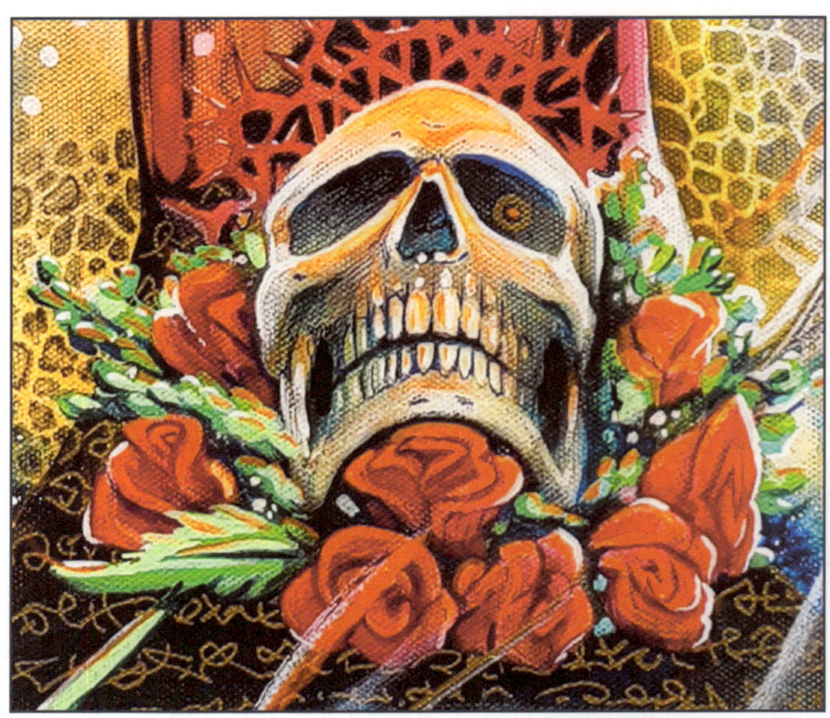

*Atonement*, 2020
24"x36"
Acrylic & Mixed Media on Canvas

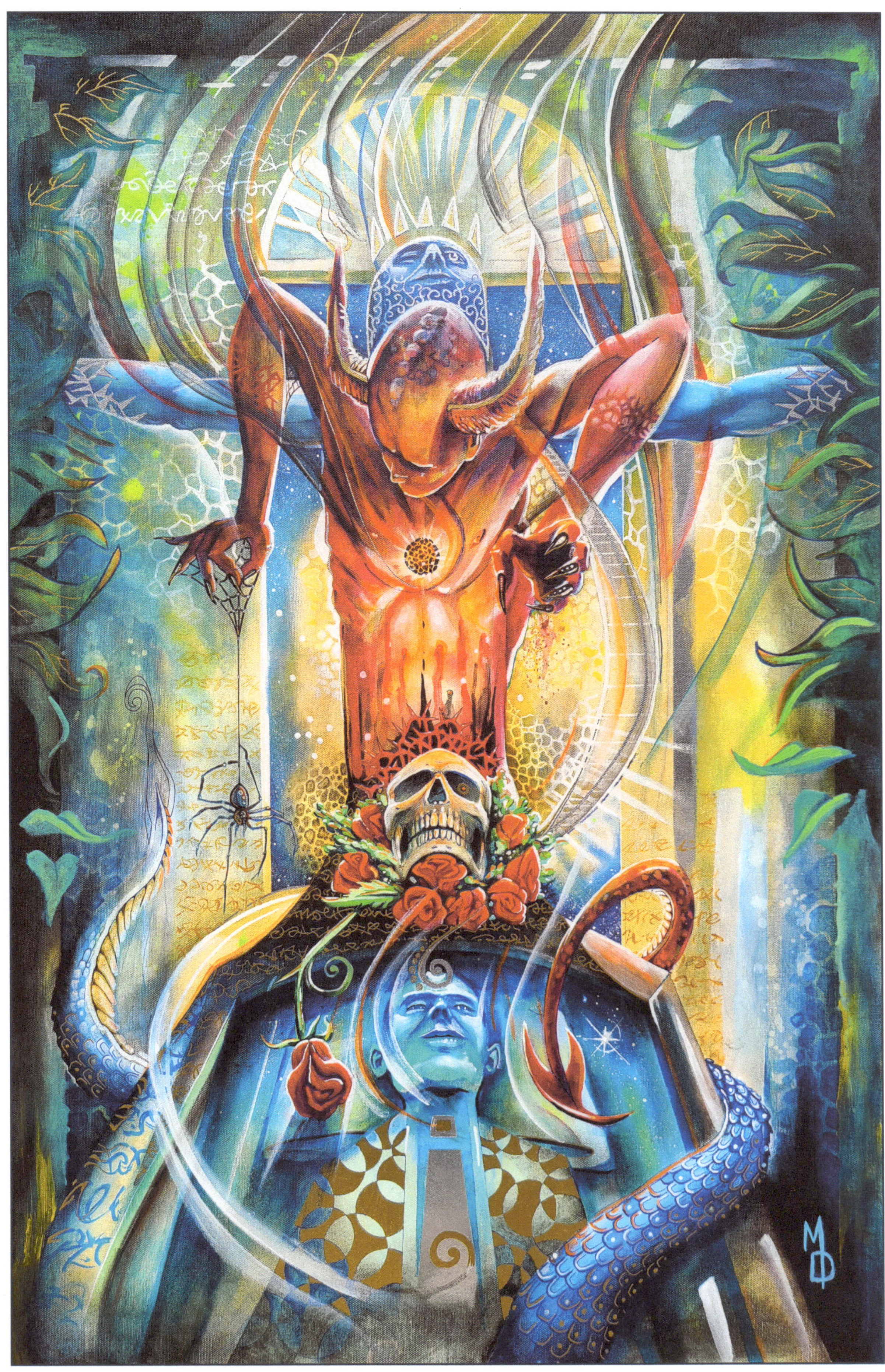

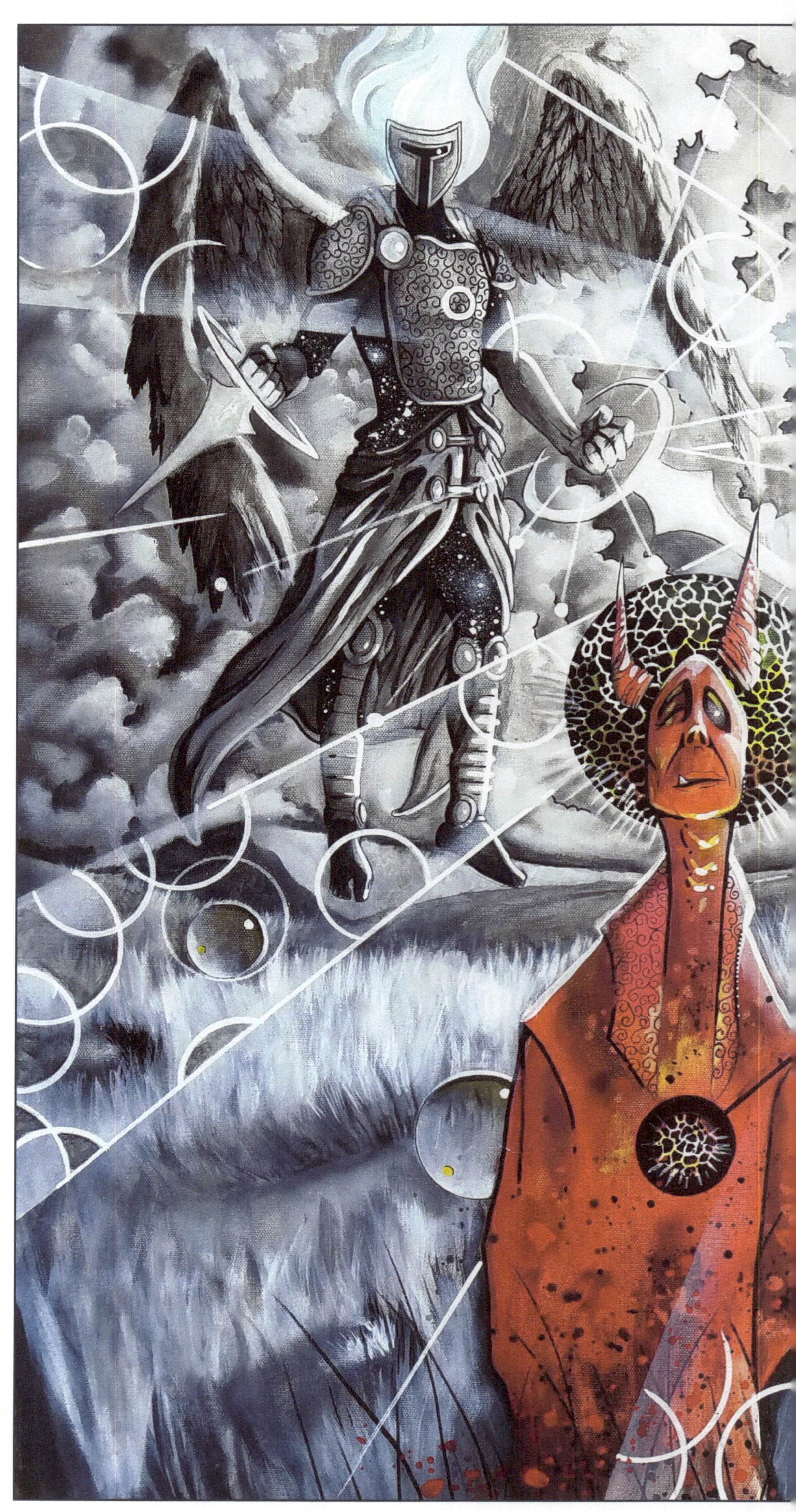

*Gravitas at the Gates*, 2018
40"x30"
Acrylic & Mixed Media on Canvas

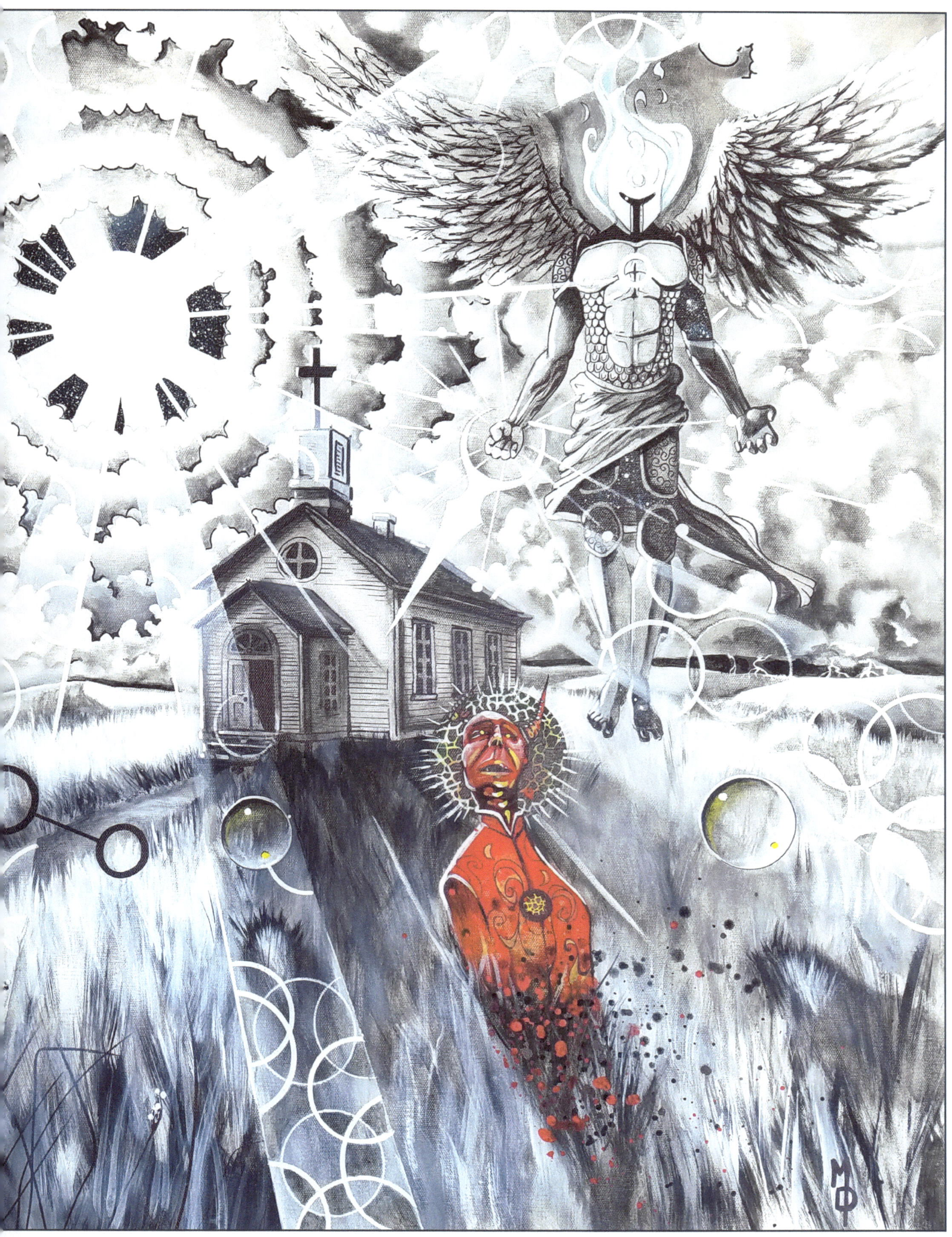

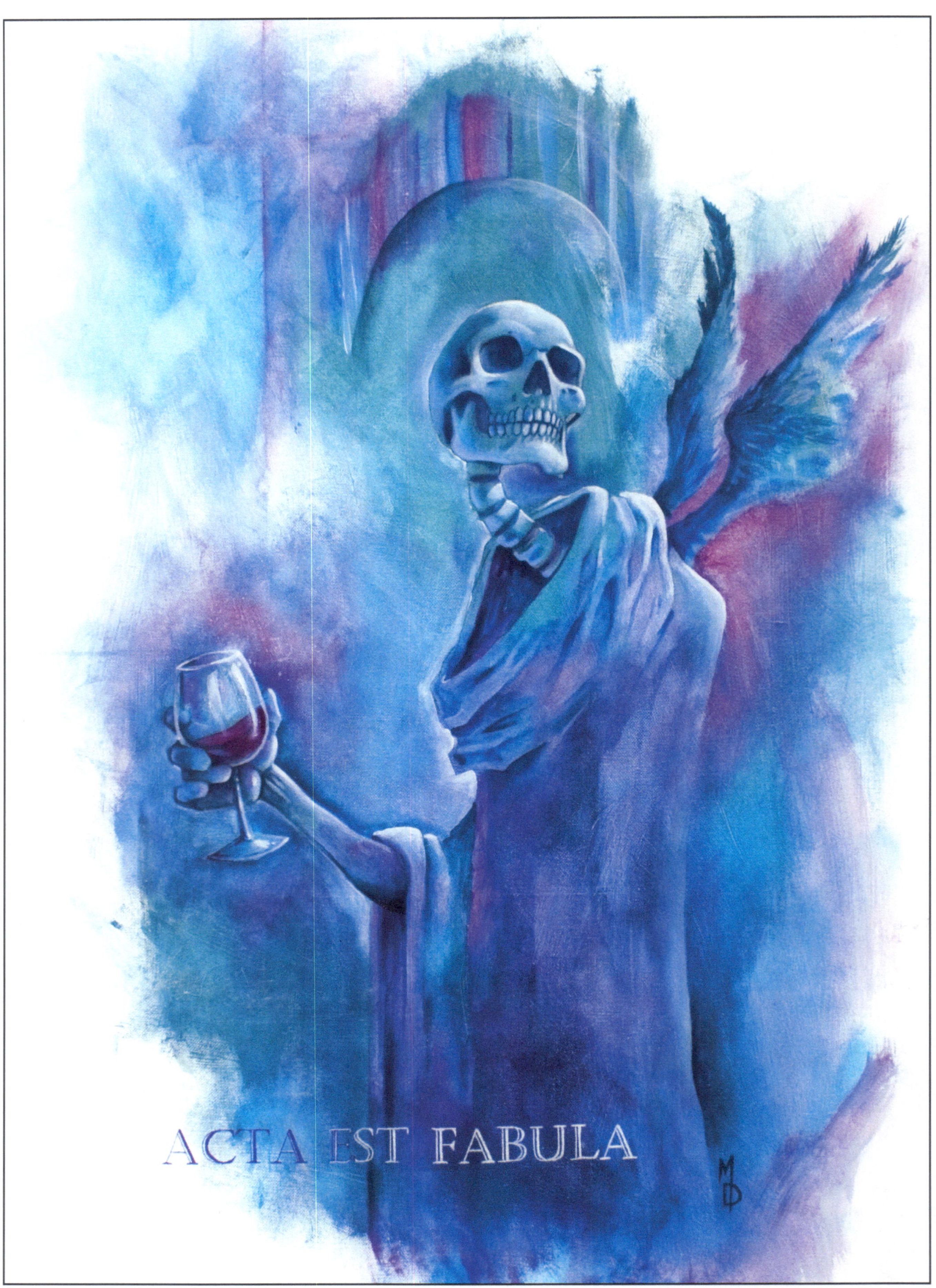
ACTA EST FABULA
MD

"I've always enjoyed exploring the idea of an 'Angel of Death' and interpretations of angels and demons. I've been discovering for myself that many times there is a yin and yang to life. No light without dark. Good and evil existing in necessary communal balance. I try rendering the Angel of Death as a divine messenger with both dark and holy characteristics."

***So the Story Ends*, 2013**
24"x36"
Acrylic & Mixed Media on Canvas

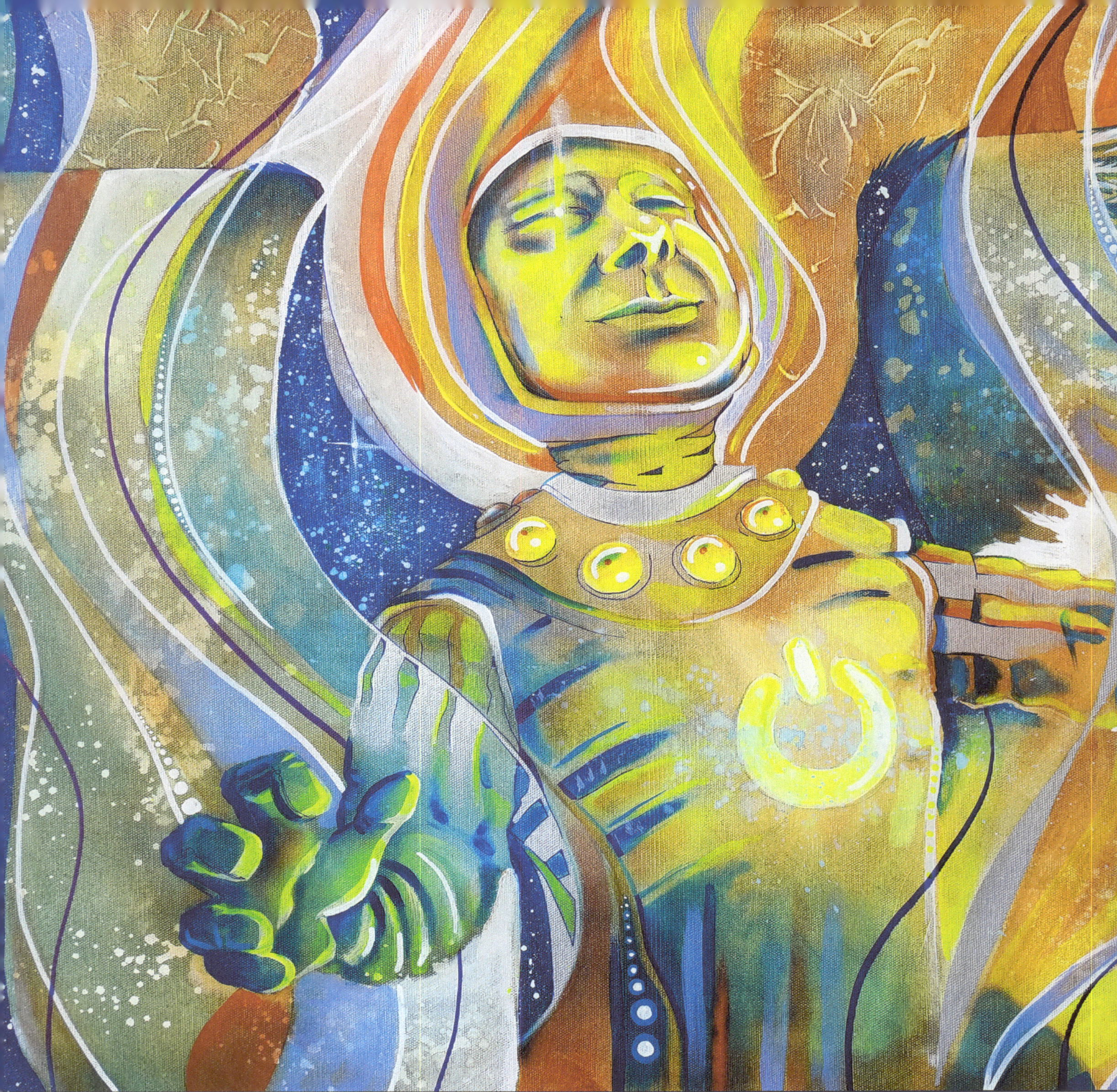

*The Wondernaut*, 2017
48"x24"
Acrylic & Mixed Media on Canvas
*Blacklight Enhanced*

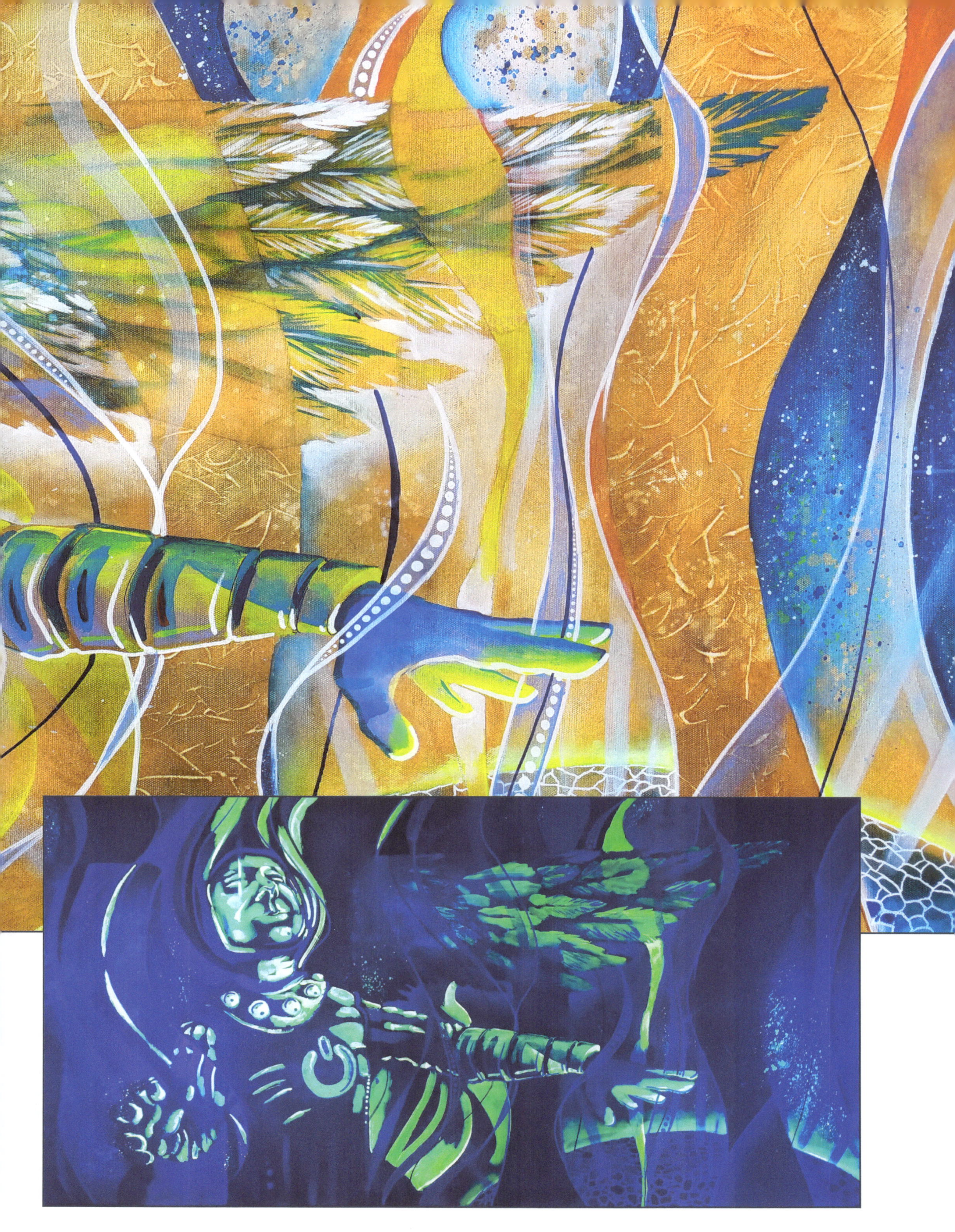

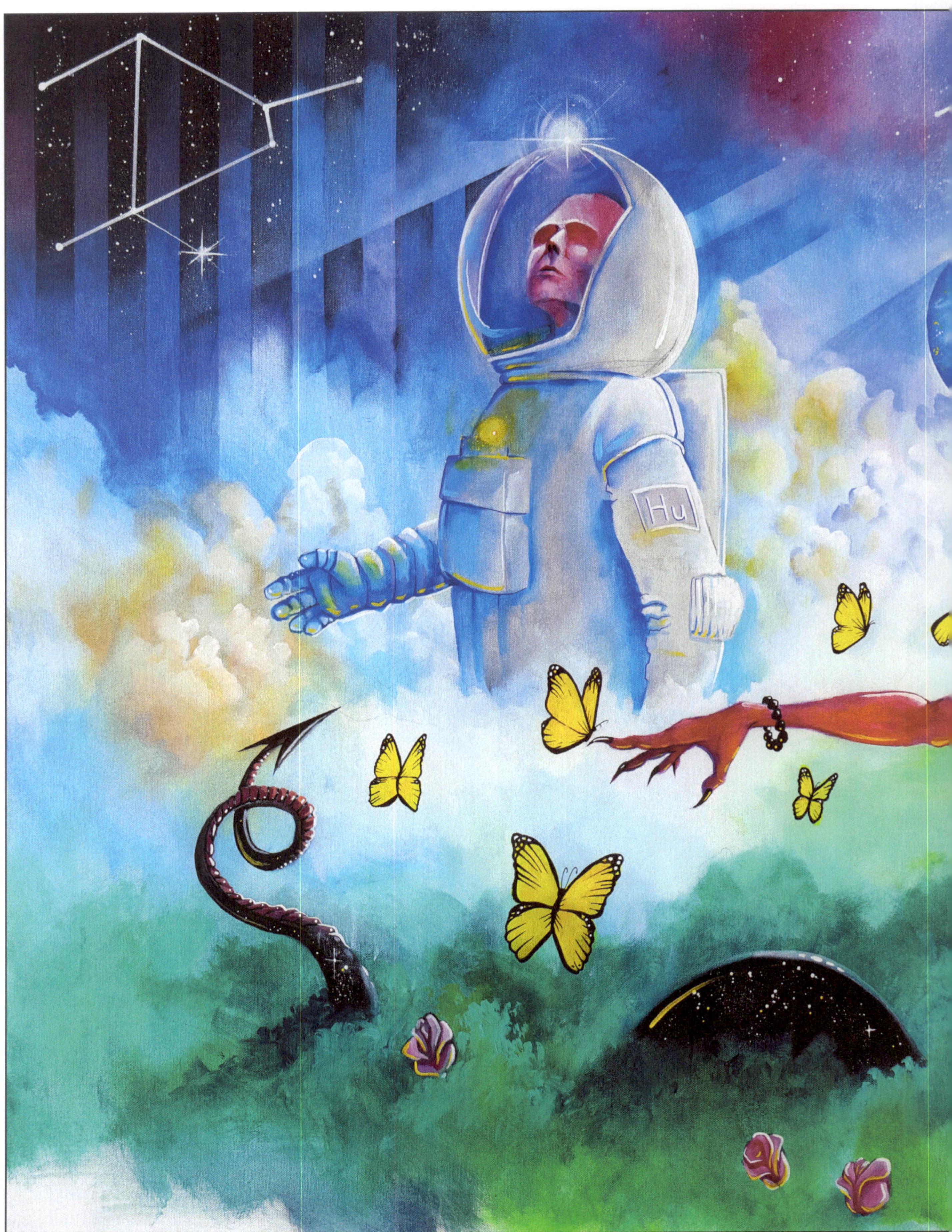
Hu

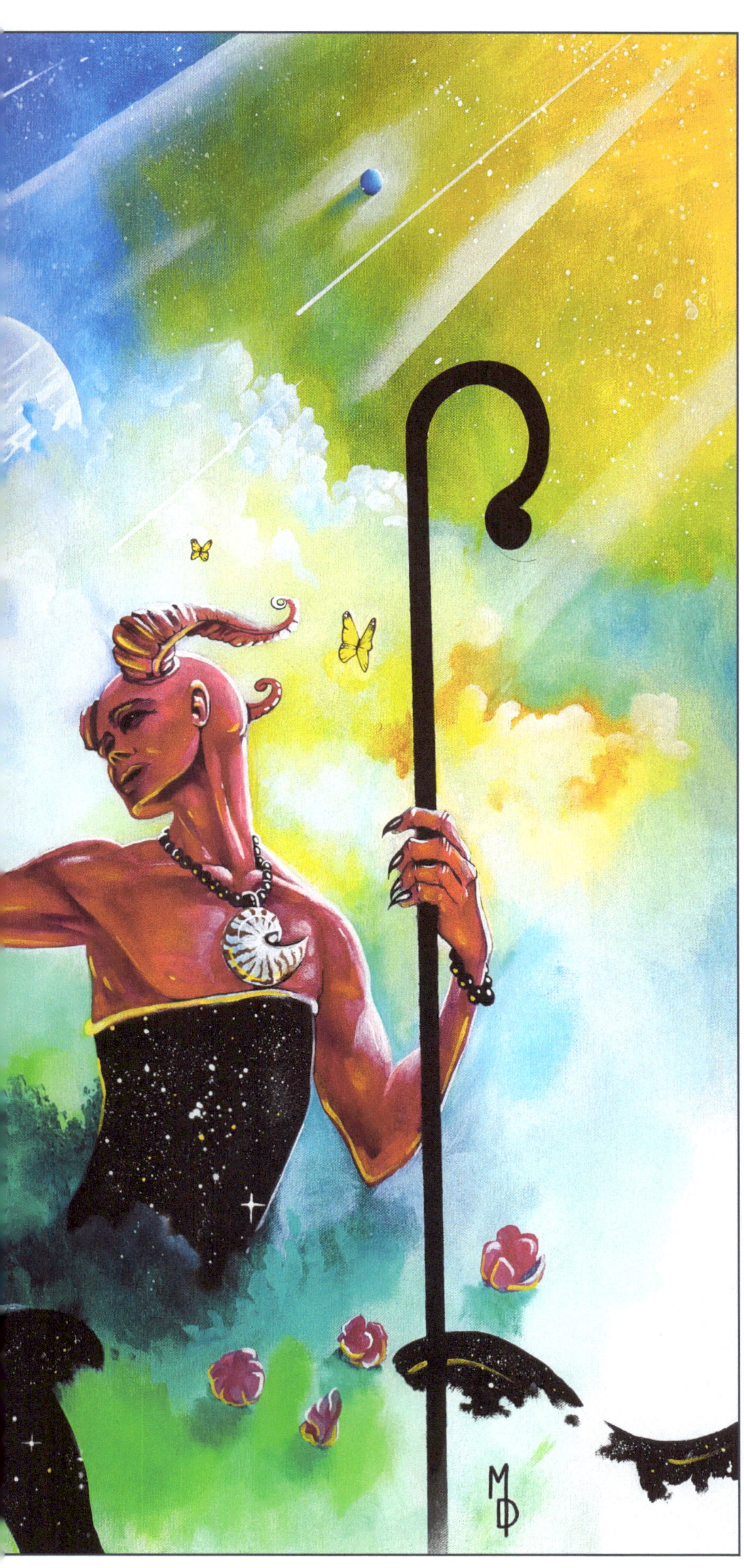

*Evolutionary*, 2016
48"x36"
Acrylic & Mixed Media on Canvas

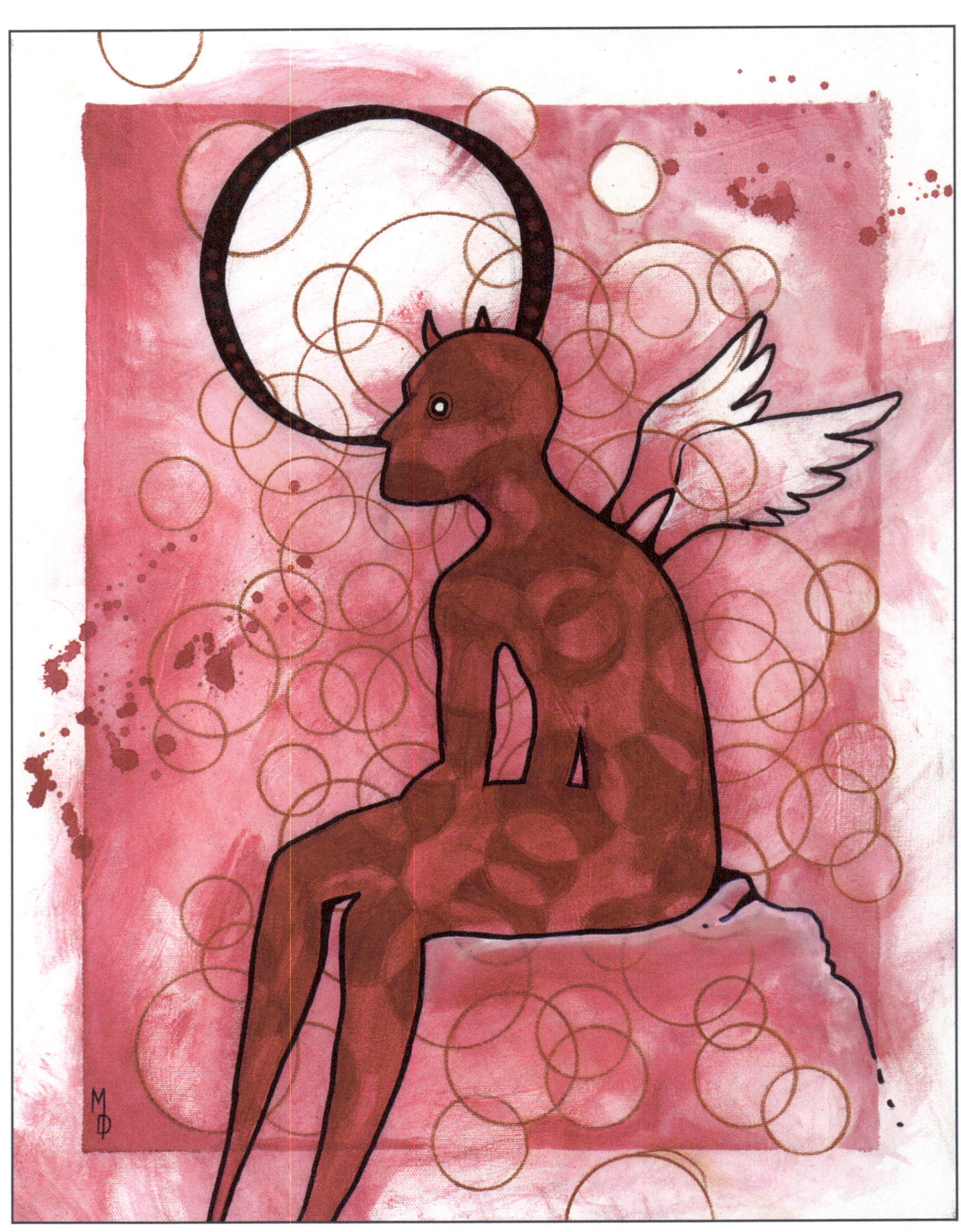

*Contemplation of Right & Wrong*, 2007
16"x20"
Acrylic & Mixed Media on Canvas

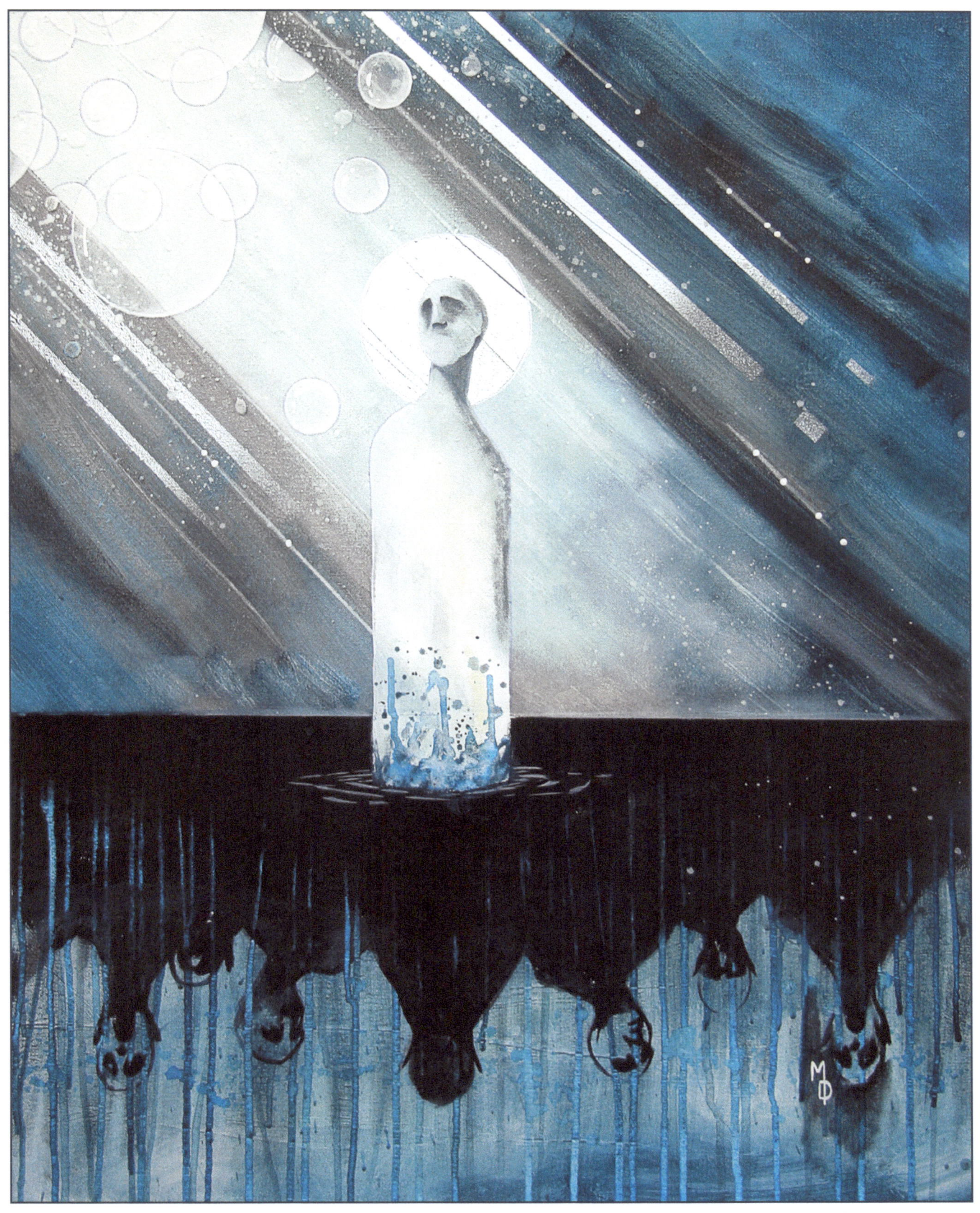


*Dark Waters*, 2009
18"x24"
Acrylic & Mixed Media on Canvas

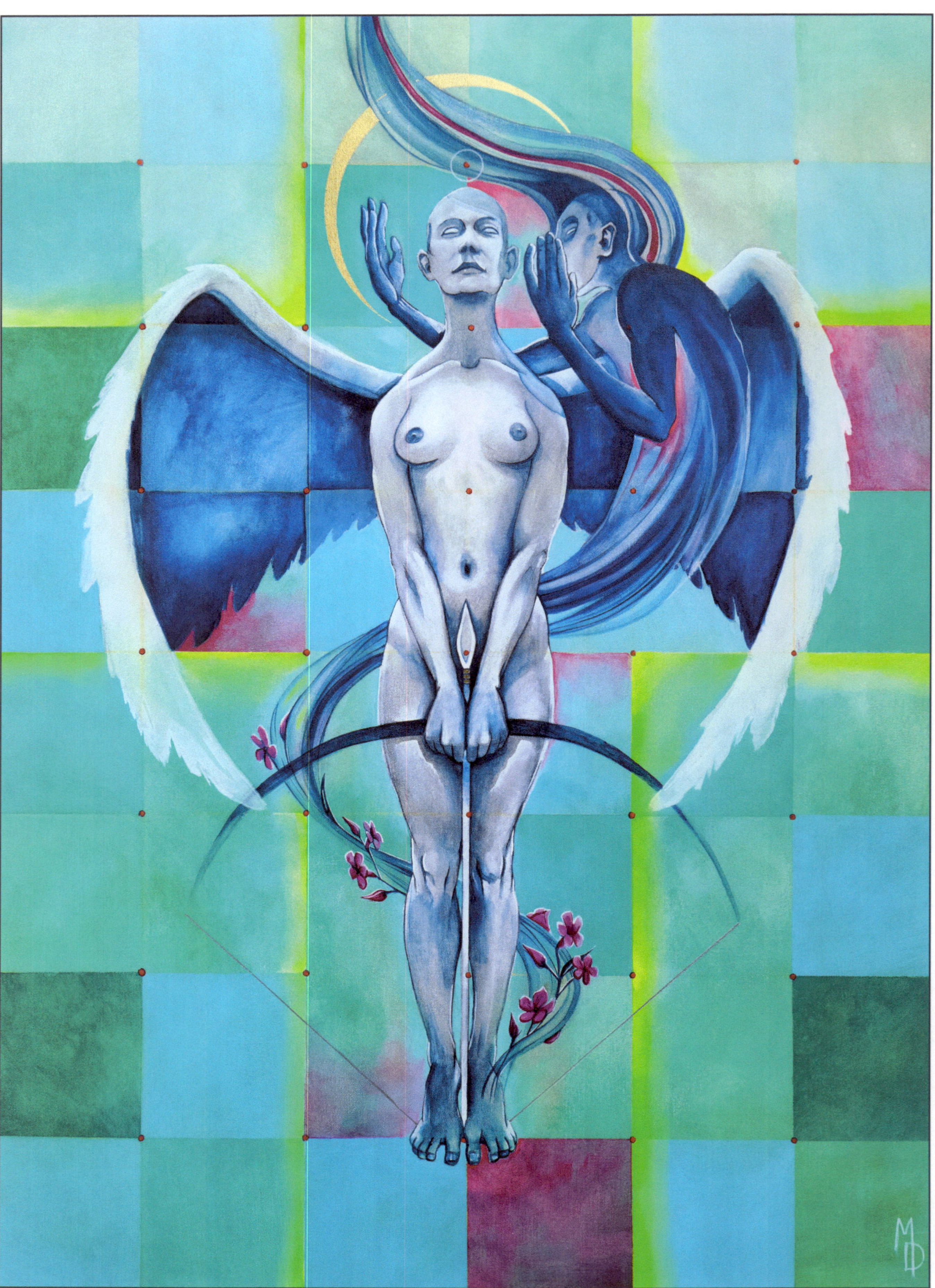

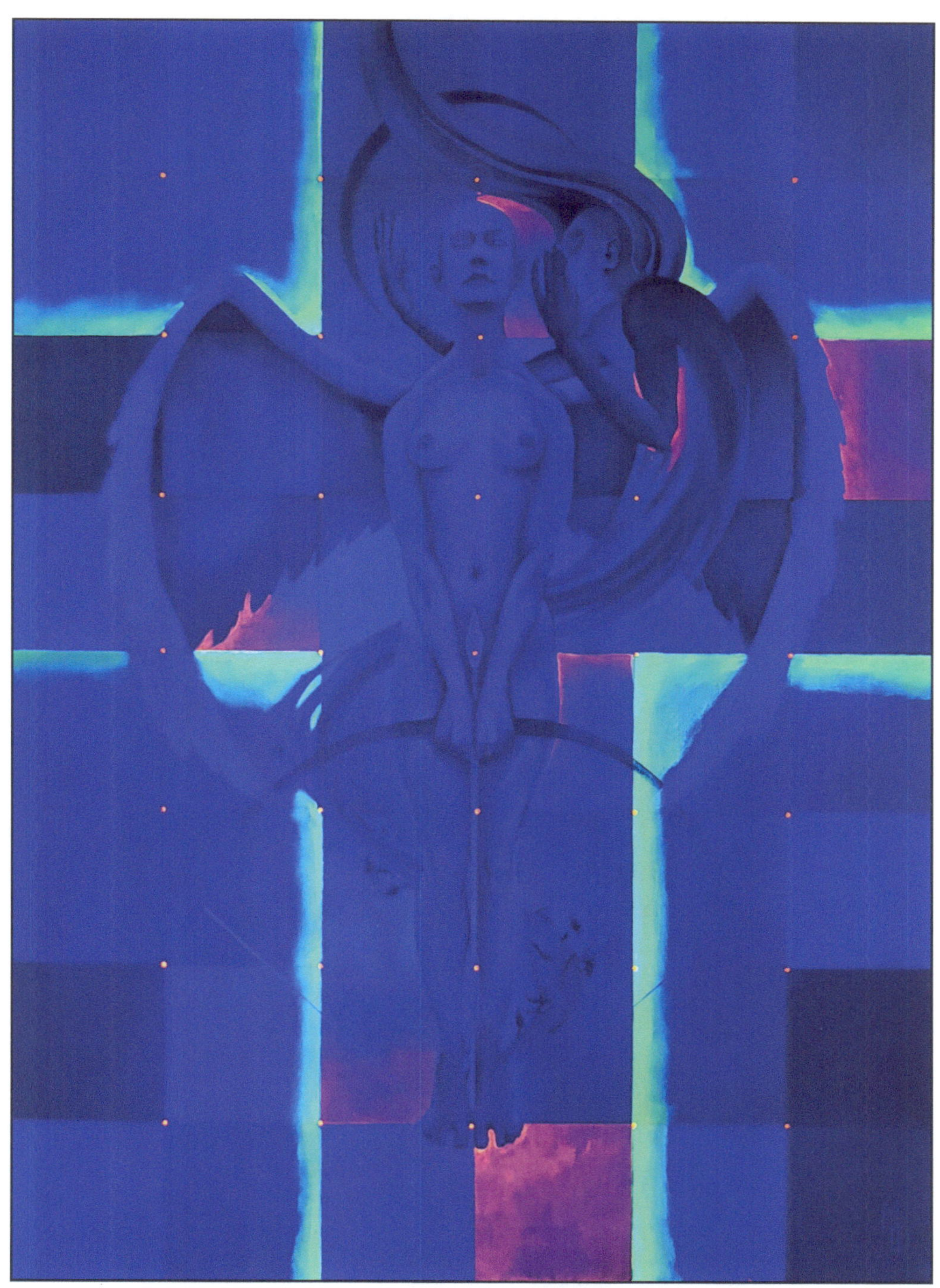

*Martyr*, 2023
30"x40"
Acrylic & Mixed Media on Canvas
*Blacklight Enhanced*

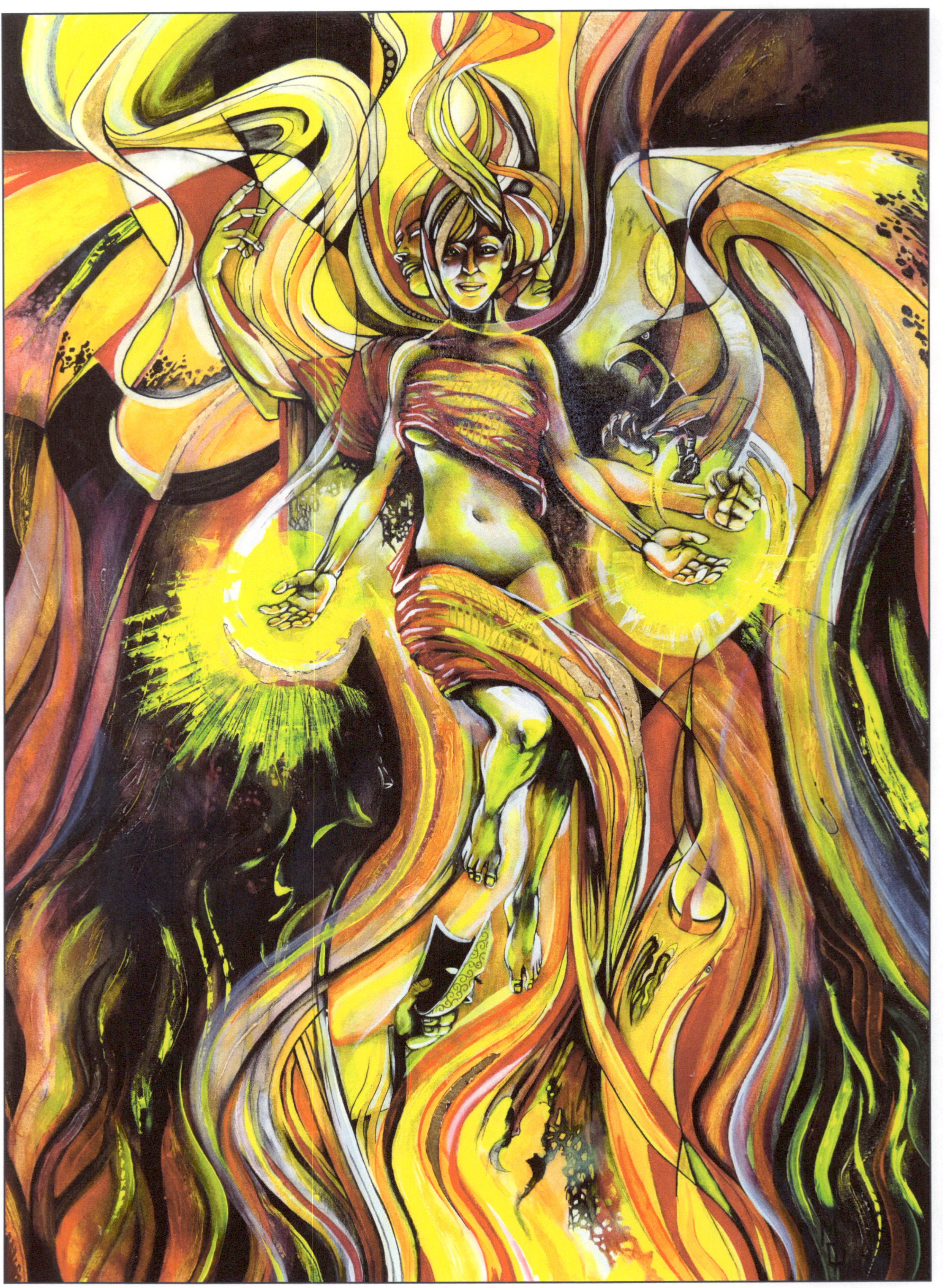

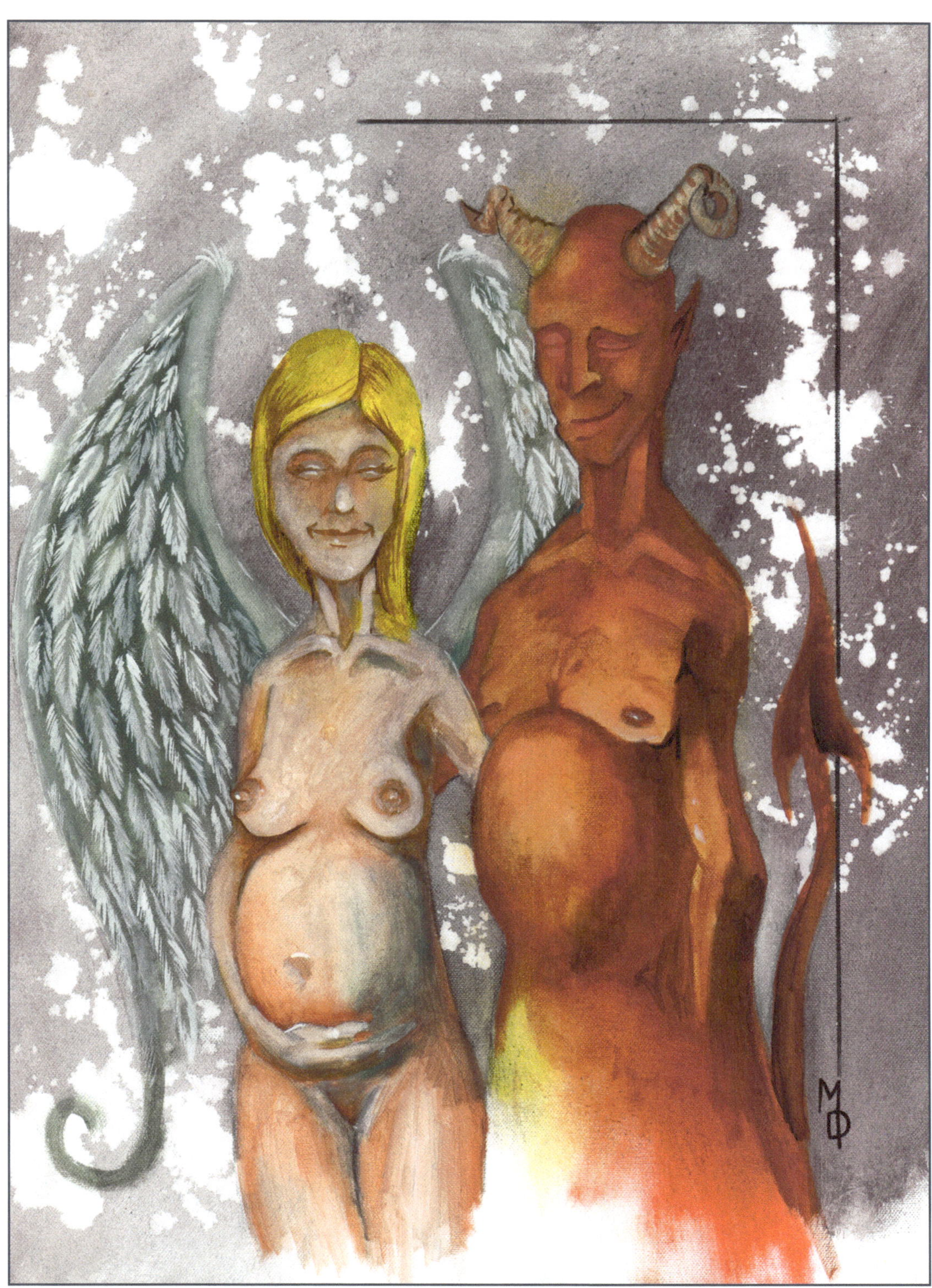

*Phoenix Rising*, 2023
30"x40"
Acrylic & Mixed Media on Canvas

*Birth of Duality*, 2010
18"x24"
Acrylic & Mixed Media on Canvas

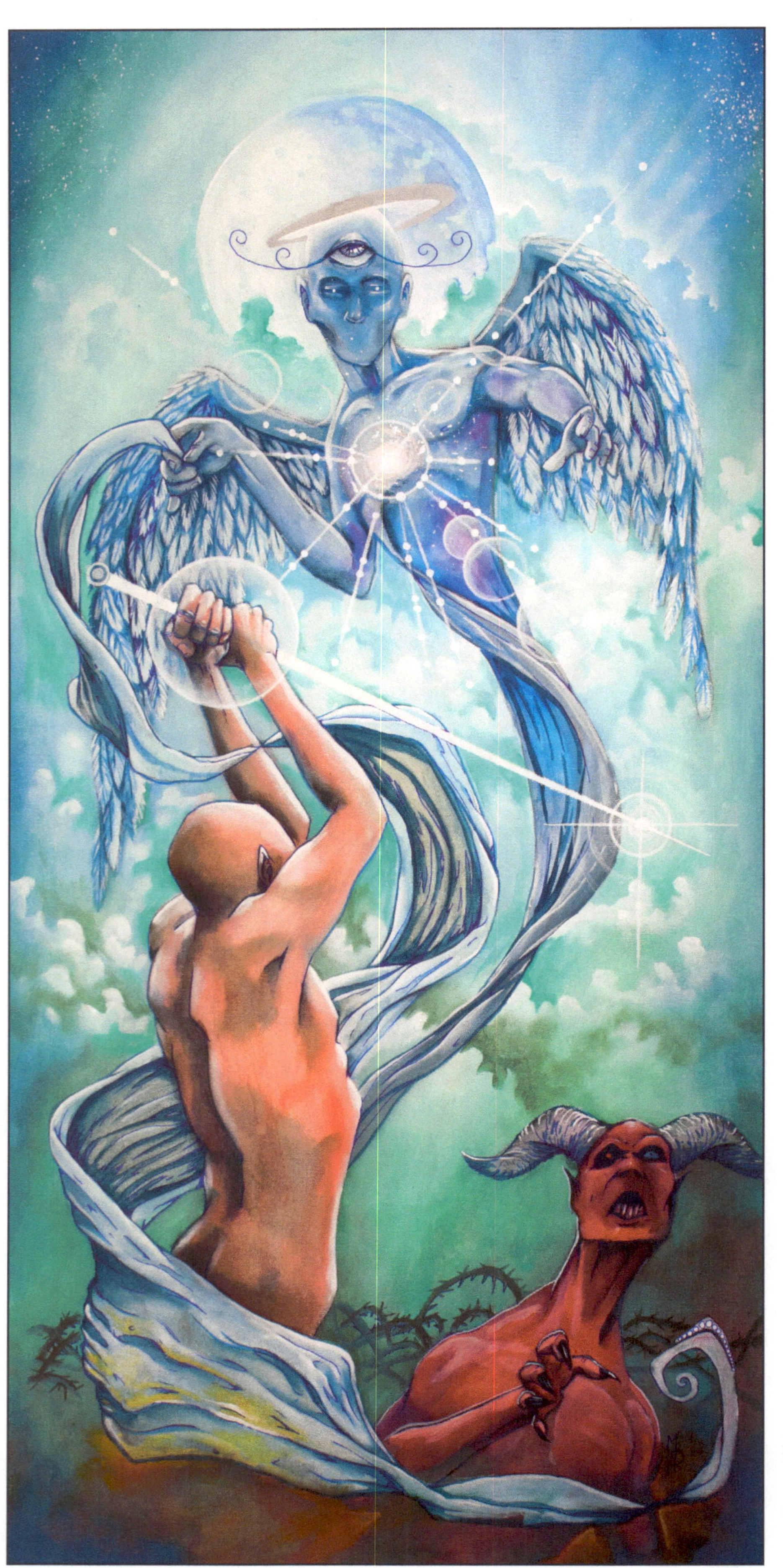

*Demon's Defeat*, 2013
18"x36"
Acrylic & Mixed Media on Canvas

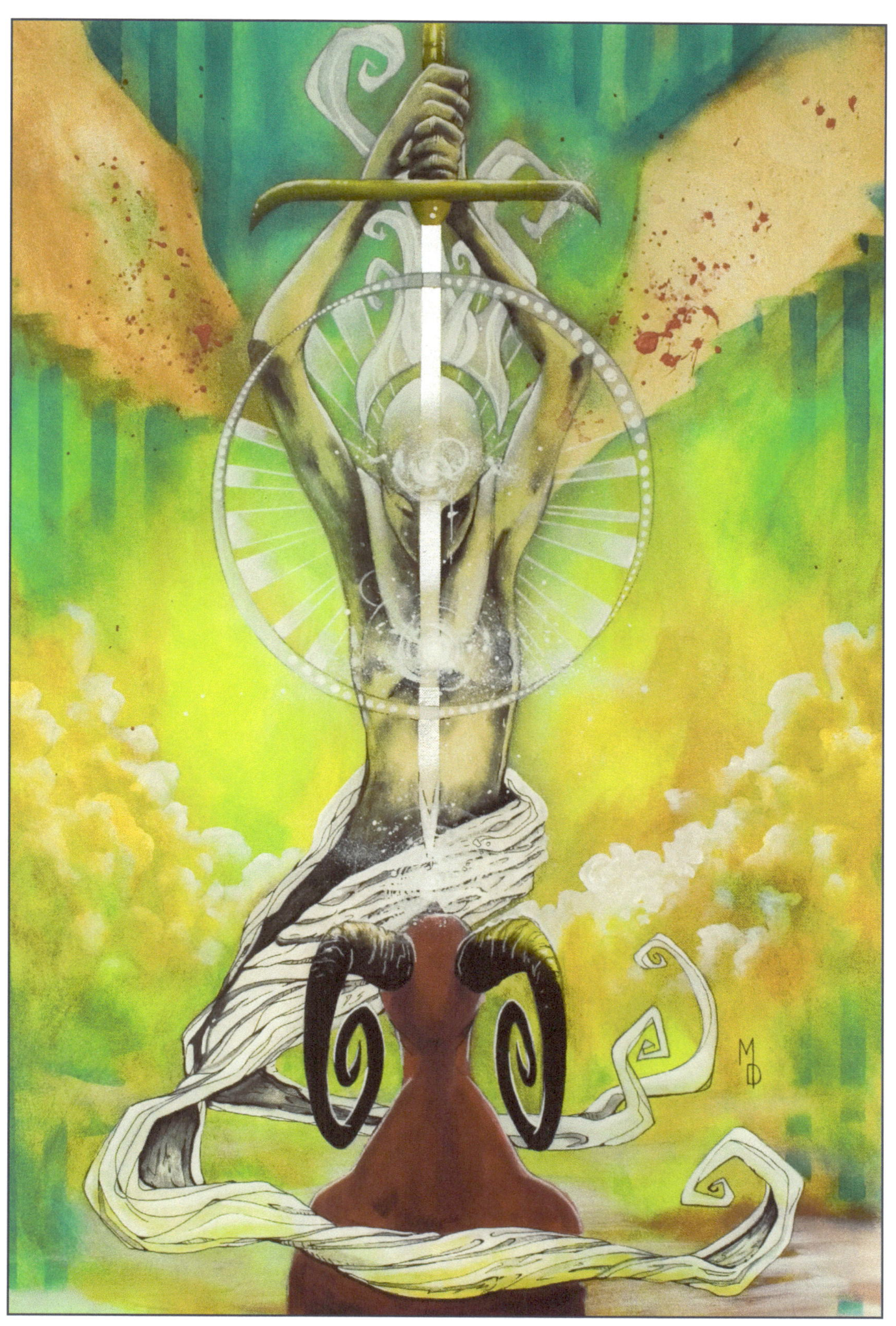

*Expulsion*, 2013
24"x36"
Acrylic & Mixed Media on Canvas

*The Rising*, 2019
30"x40"
Acrylic & Mixed Media on Canvas

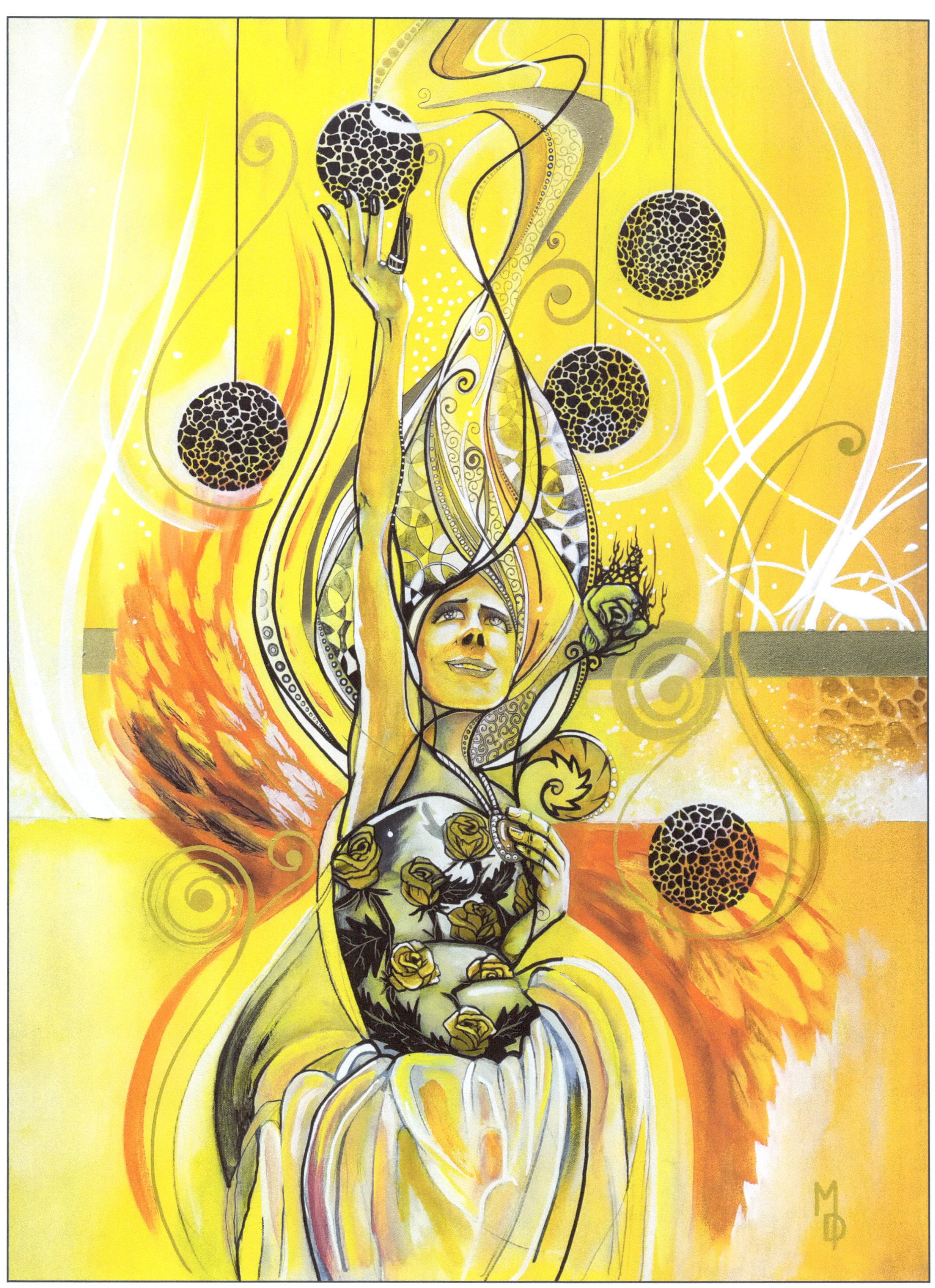

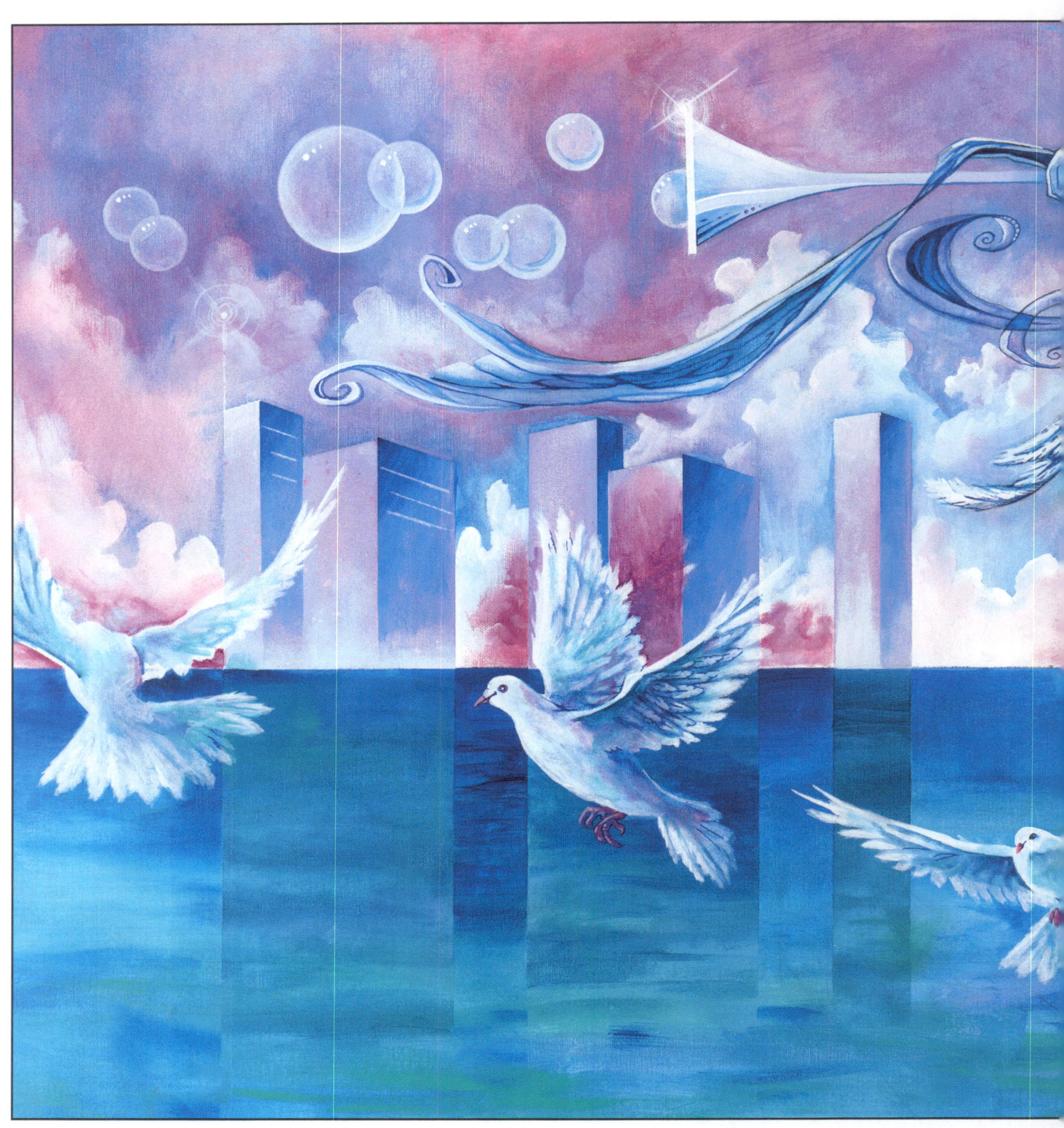

*Launch Forth into the Deep*, 2013
48"x24"
Acrylic & Mixed Media on Canvas

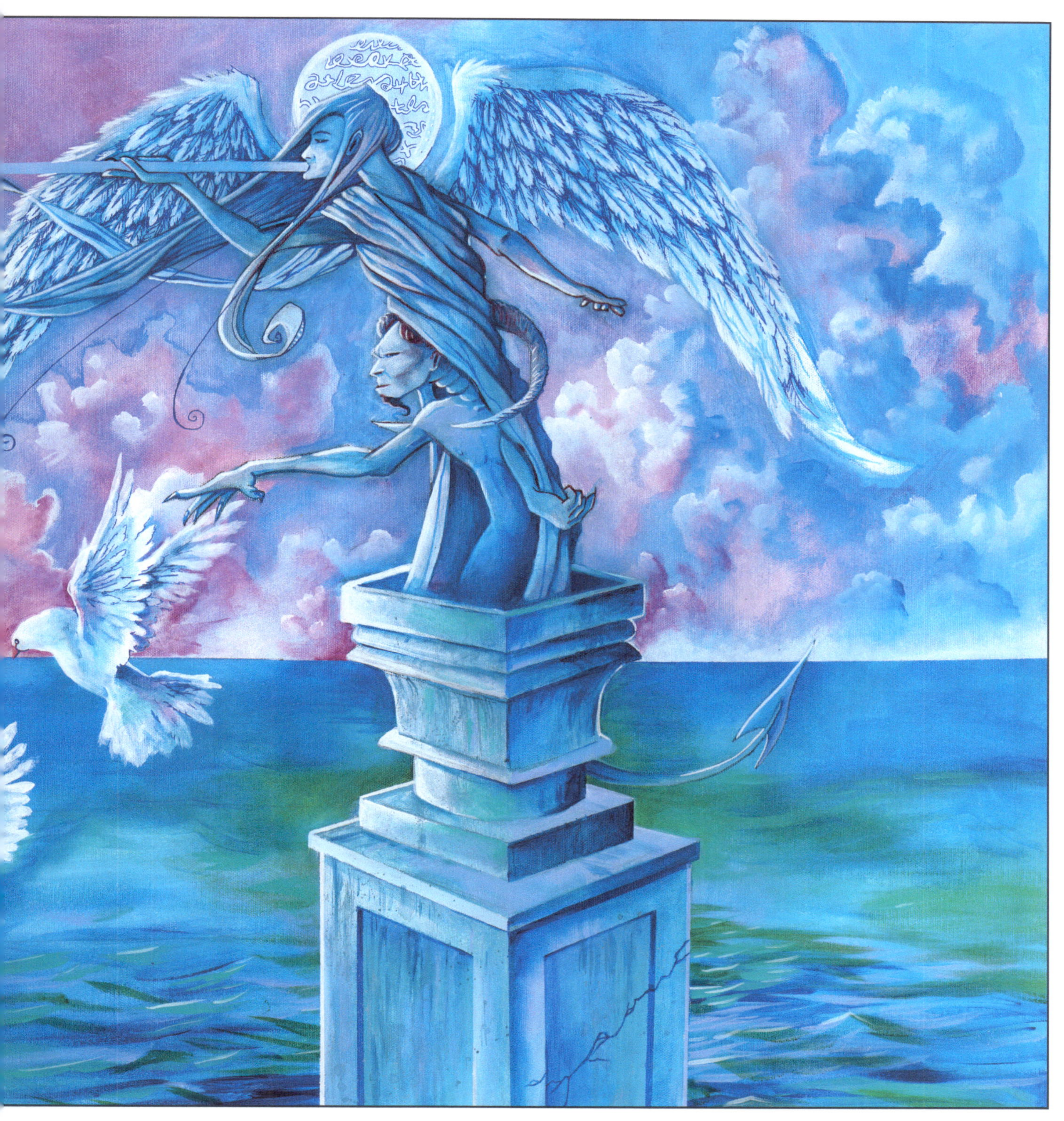

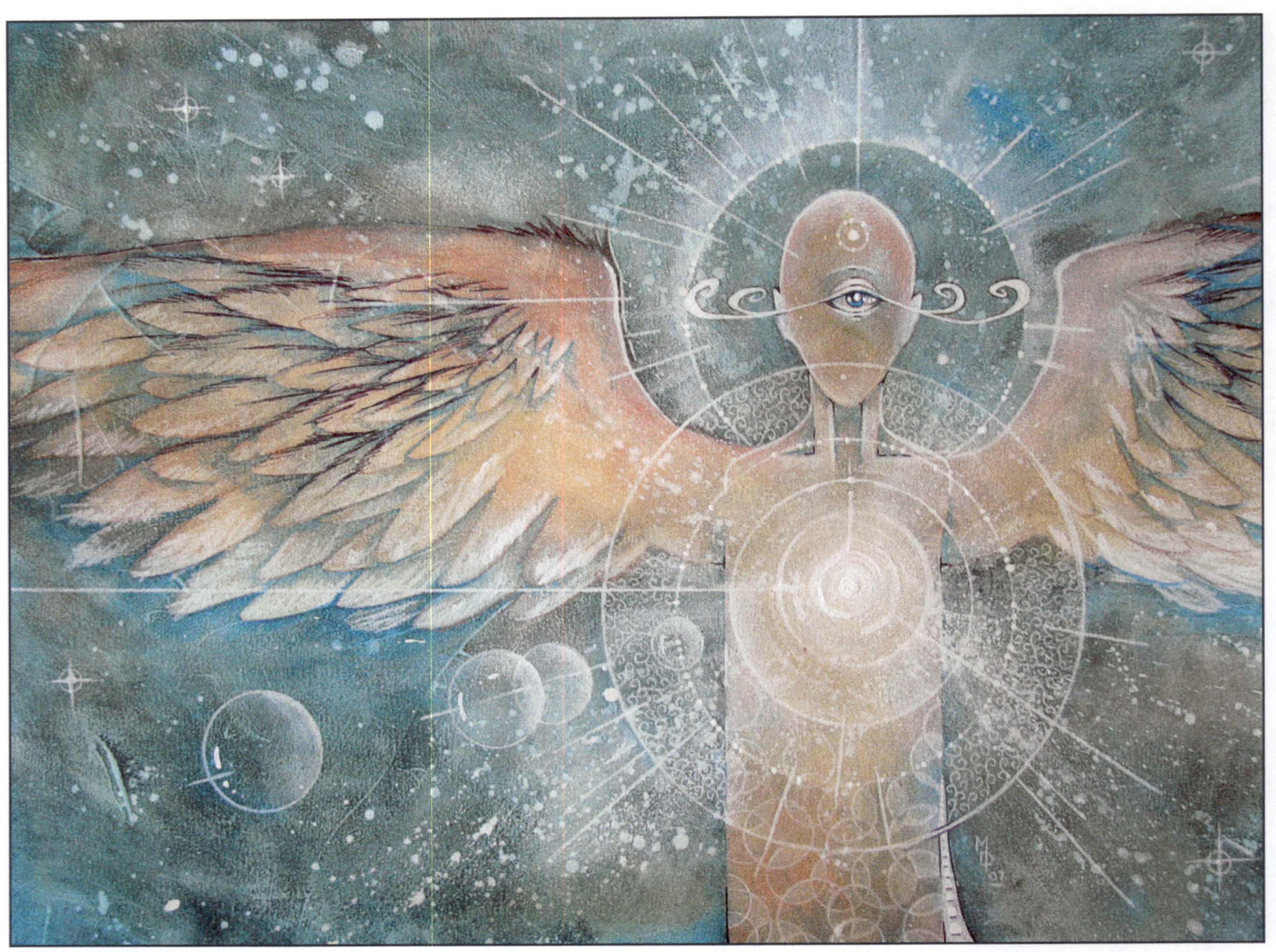

*Cycloptic Angel*, 2007
29"x21"
Acrylic & Mixed Media on Paper

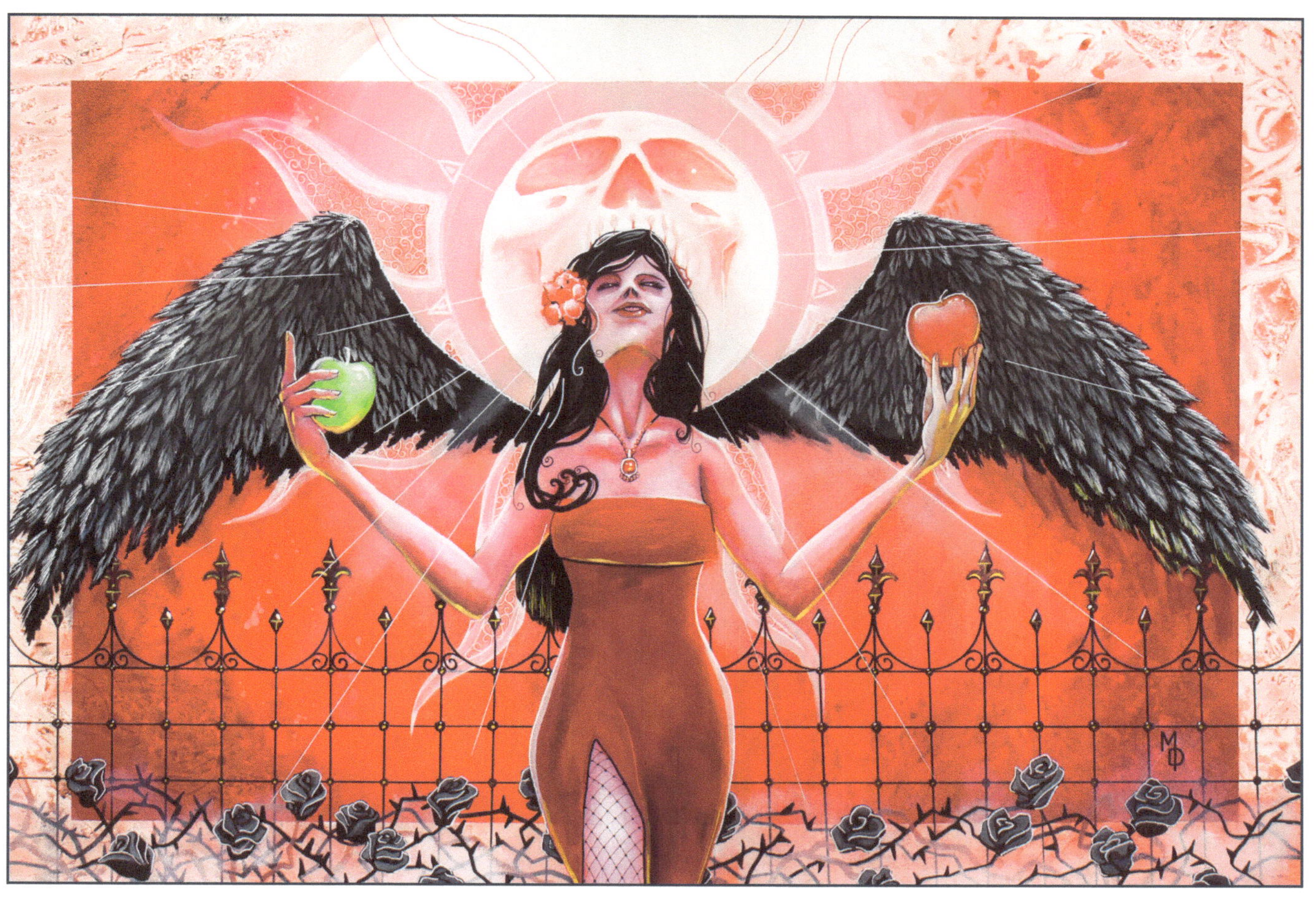

*Temptress*, 2015
36"x24"
Acrylic & Mixed Media on Canvas

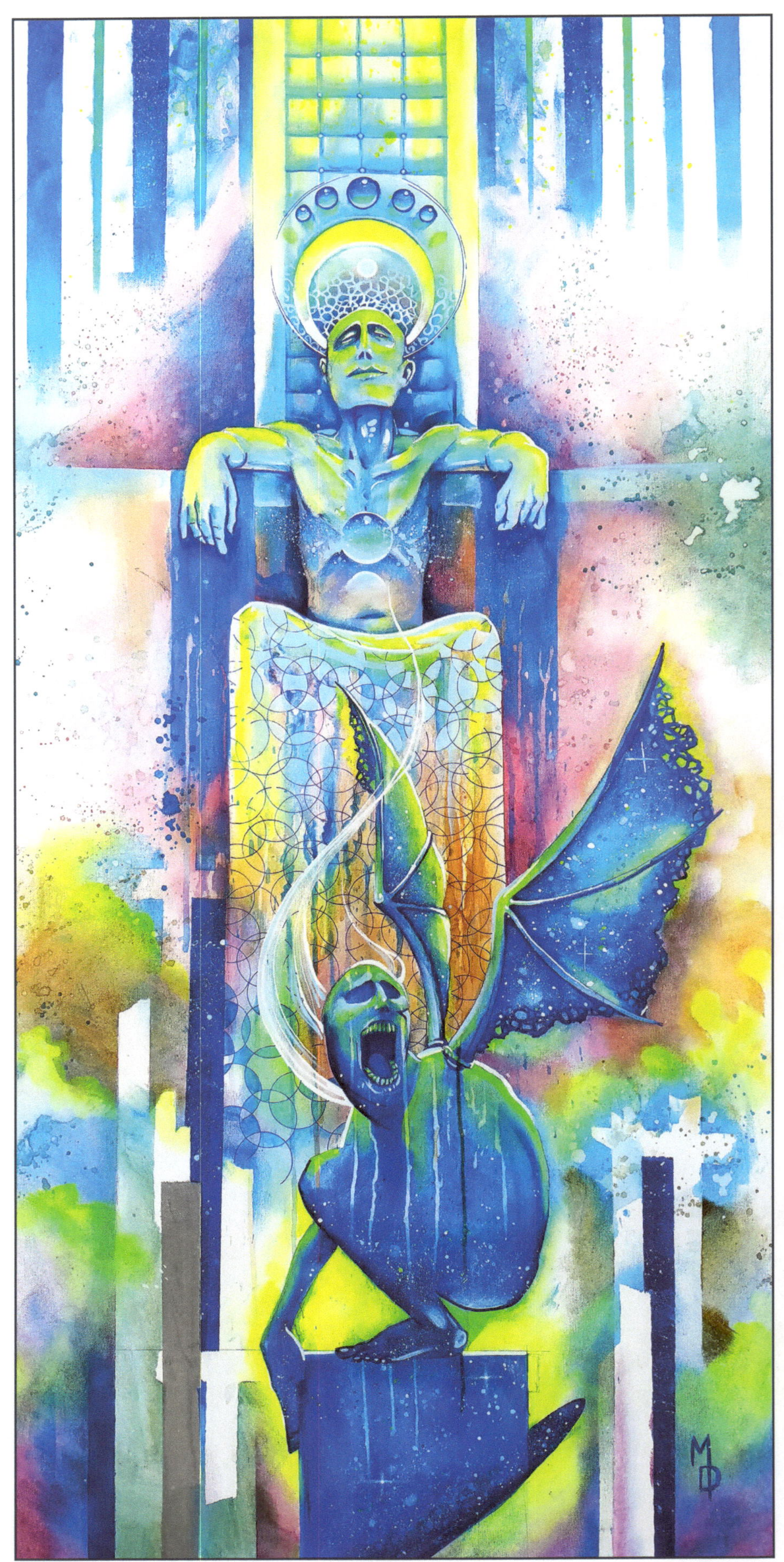

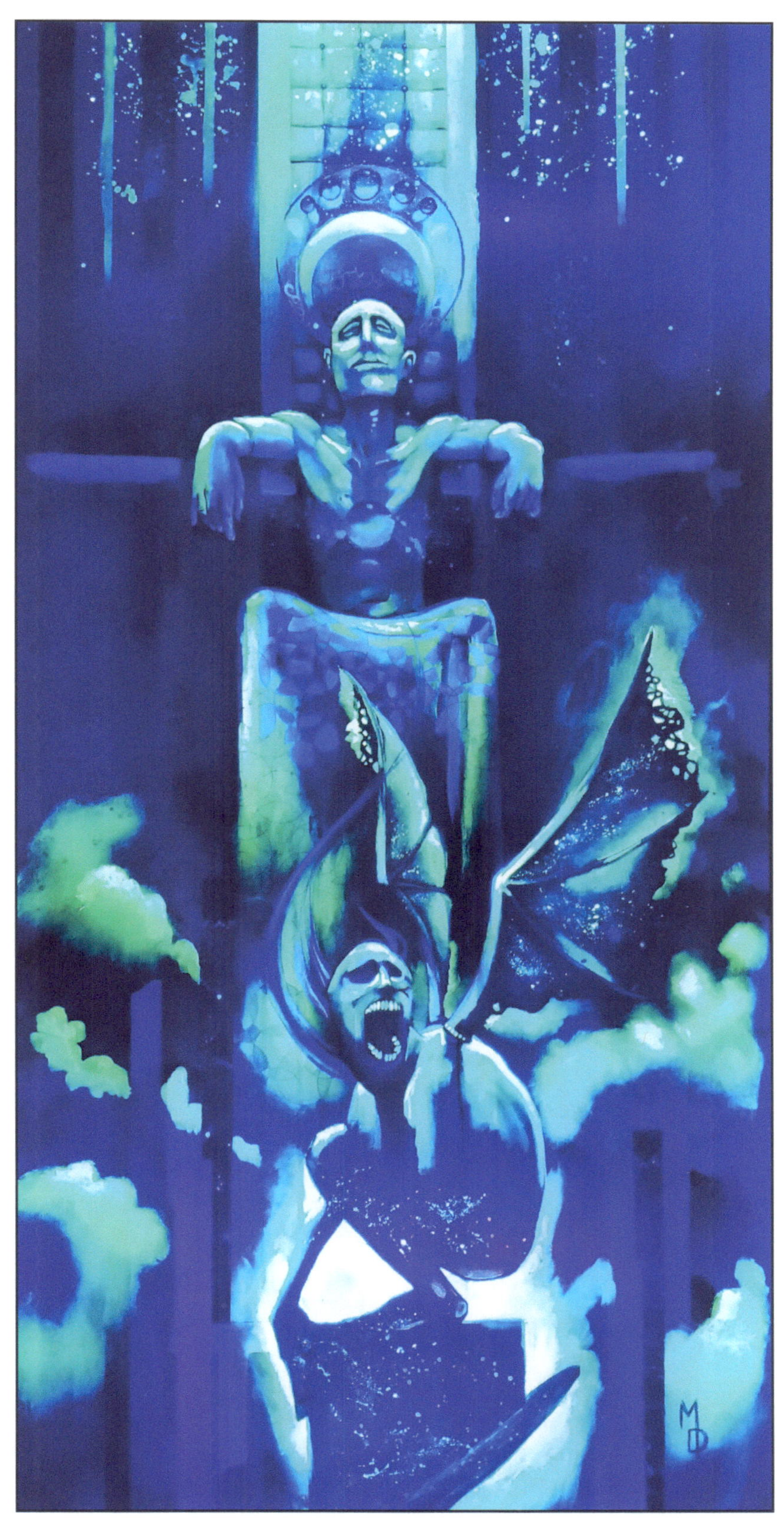

*The Beast Beneath*, 2017
24"x48"
Acrylic & Mixed Media on Canvas
*Blacklight Enhanced*

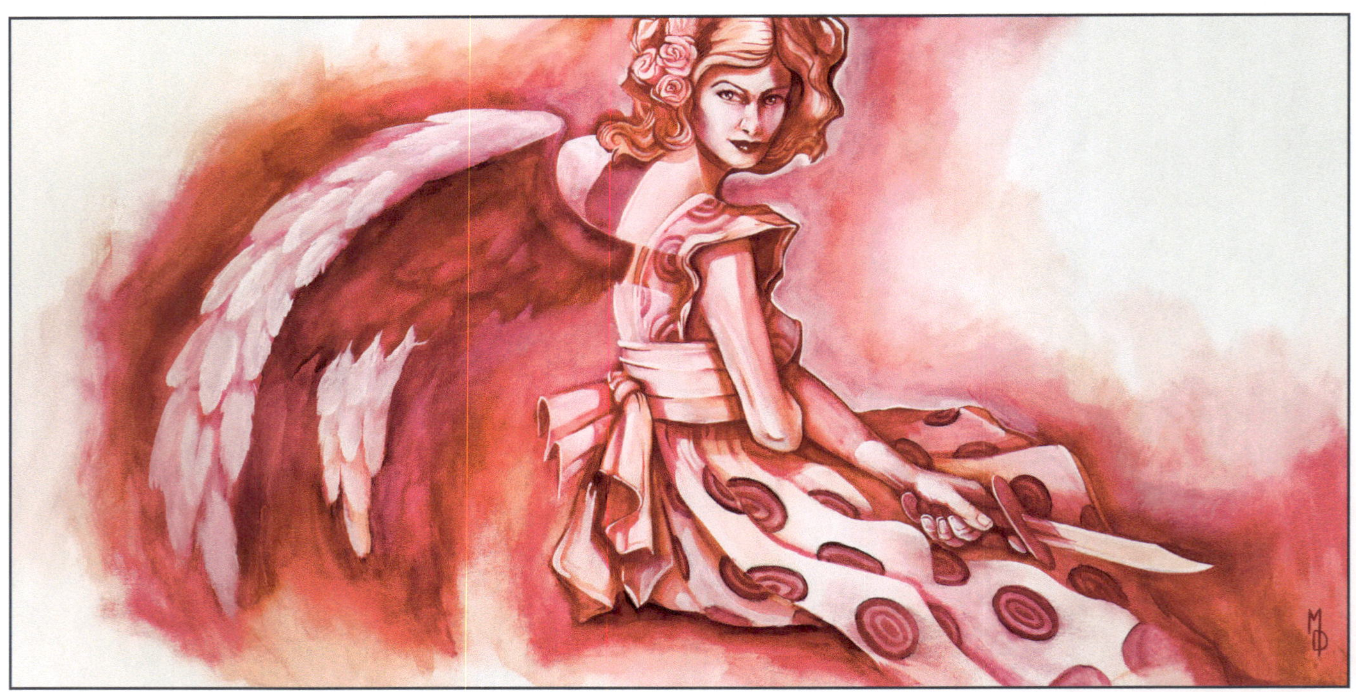

*Gargoyle*, 2022
48"x24"
Acrylic & Mixed Media on Canvas

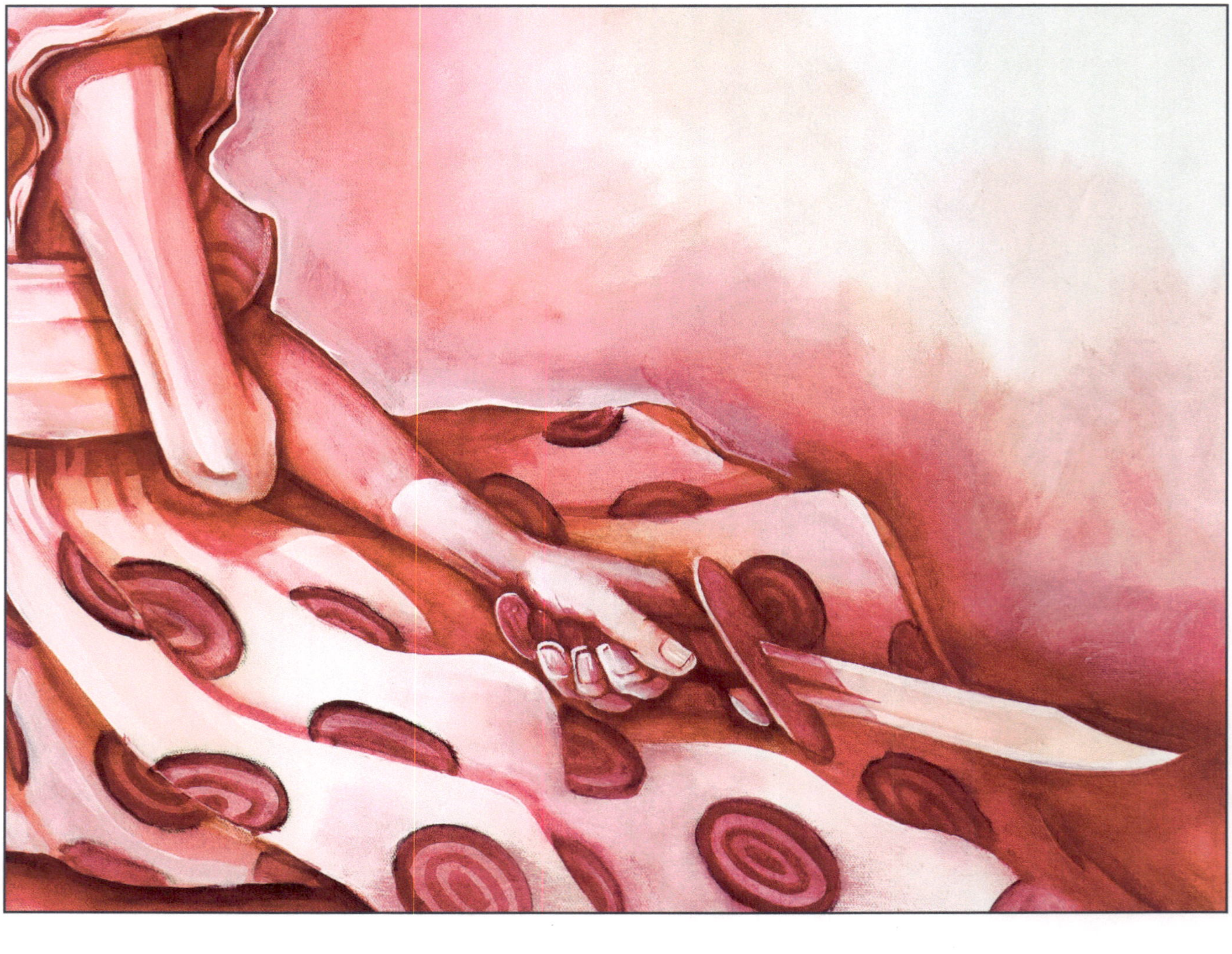

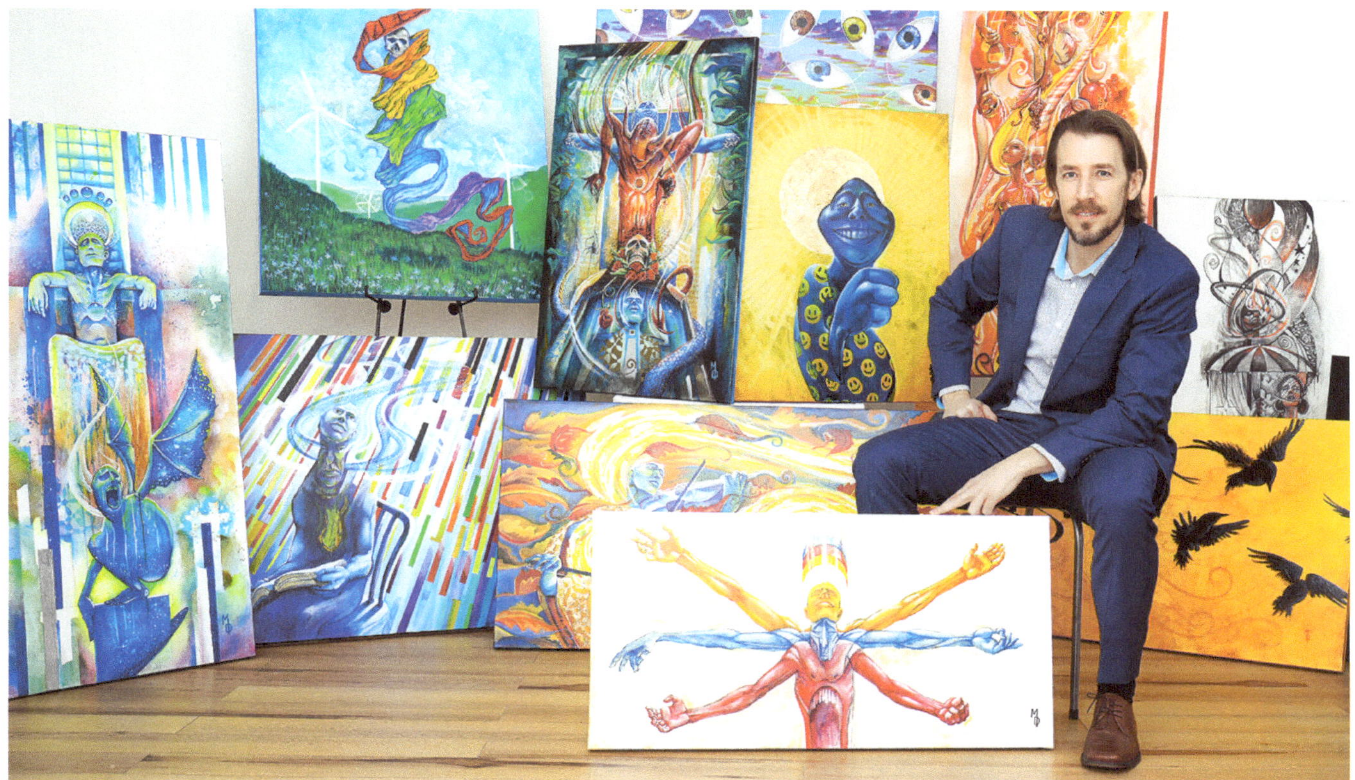

# Miles Davis

Through painting, Miles explores the crossroads of modern spirituality and science and seeks to examine those complexities in an honest way. Inspired by the evolving relationship between personal and cultural identity, he uses crisp illustrative aesthetics and dramatic symbolism to engage the viewer. Striving for a unique accessibility, Miles endeavors to bypass perceived elitist tendencies and create work that speaks to everyone despite their art education.

Since 2003, Miles has been building his art practice through personal work, commissions, and public art. He has been included in grant projects from the National Endowment for the Arts and has received numerous awards for his paintings. Miles exhibits both nationally and internationally and made his debut solo museum exhibition in 2022 with "Vibrant Shadows" at the Marietta Cobb Museum of Art. For more information on Miles and his work, explore the other books in the Studio Collections series and visit massiveburn.com.

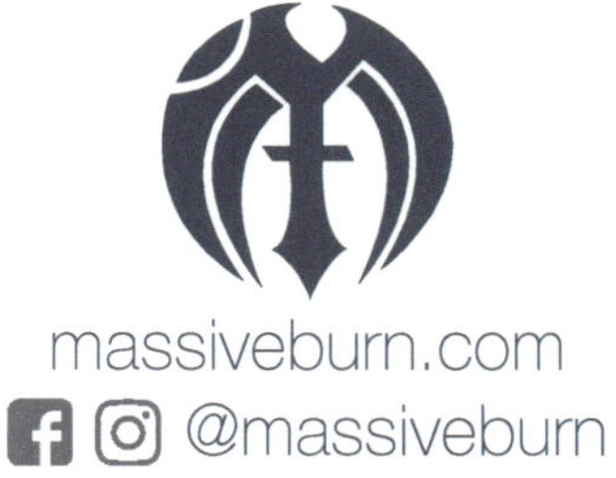

massiveburn.com

@massiveburn

www.ingramcontent.com/pod-product-compliance
Lightning Source LLC
LaVergne TN
LVHW070153110826
845147LV00002B/386
* 9 7 9 8 9 9 1 8 8 1 6 1 6 *